#Fake You -
An Activist's Guide to Defeating Disinformation

Simona Levi et al.

AF406991

Don't blame the people, don't blame the Internet.
Blame the power

Governments, political parties, mass media large corporations and fortunes: the monopolies of information manipulation and the threats to freedom of expression.

Please share by all means :)

A project directed by Simona Levi

The core text is the adaptation and update of #FakeYou - Fake news y desinformación - Gobiernos, partidos políticos, medios de comunicación de masas, corporaciones, grandes fortunas: monopolios de la manipulación informativa y recortes de la libertad de expresión, Ediciones Rayo Verde, 2019.
By Simona Levi with core contributions from Xnet, Guillem Martínez, Max Carbonell*, Gemma Palau*, Elizabeth Bodi* and Gemma García Rams*, Lorin Decarli and Tatiana Bazzichelli, Emanuele Cozzo, Luce Prignano, Robert Guixaró, Natàlia Ribés*, Marta Timón*, Cristina Cabasés*, Alberto Martín*, Ximo Blasco*.

Other advisors:
Miriam Carles, Sergio Salgado, Mariluz Congosto, Felipe Fonseca, Paulo José Lara, Alberto Escorcia, Stephen Armstrong, Renata Avila, Anne Koch, Biella Coleman, Cory Doctorow, Wu Ming, Biffud, Nick Komninos, Christopher Millard, different types of AI.

In collaboration with the Andrew Wainwright Reform Trust, Culture Institute of Barcelona City Council and General Directorate for the Promotion and Defence of Human Rights of Generalitat de Catalunya.

*As core researchers in the framework of the postgraduate course on Technopolitics and Rights in the Digital Age at BSM–Pompeu Fabra University (and University of Barcelona), directed by Simona Levi and Cristina Ribas.

Editor: Jon Potter.

Design: Tono Cristòfol, Irene Landa

Edited by Xnet.
ISBN: 978-84-09-63110-0
CC 4.0 licence BY-SA https://creativecommons.org/licenses/by-sa/4.0/deed.en

Barcelona, July 2024

Simona Levi

Simona Levi is a woman of action. In 2017, Rolling Stone magazine chose her as one of the 25 people shaping the future.

She is a techno-political strategist, theatre director and activist. Since 2006, she has focused on rights and democracy in the digital age, including free speech, privacy, whistleblowers, algorithmic justice, democratic governance, etc.

She founded citizen action devices such as Xnet (Institute for Democratic Digitalization and Digital Rights), # Arithmética20N, and 15Mparato. The latter has promoted the Bankia case and brought to light the black card scandal, leading to the conviction of 65 politicians and bankers, of whom 15 were imprisoned. Among them is Rodrigo Rato, the former Minister of Economy of Spain and former President of the International Monetary Fund.

As coordinator of Xnet, she studies legislation and organises action and dissemination plans so that civil society is heard, has its rights respected and has the tools to act. She designs and co-directs the Postgraduate Course in Technopolitics and Rights in the Digital Age, first at the Pompeu Fabra University, then at the University of Barcelona. She is and has been a disseminator in the media and advisor for countless citizen organisations and institutions, such as the Secretary of State for Digitalisation and Artificial Intelligence of the Government of Spain, the Directorate of Digital Society and the General Directorate of Digital Administration of the Generalitat of Catalonia. She has been a member of the advisory group of both institutions, working to draft the Charter for Digital Rights.

She is the coordinator and author of several books, such [Titles translated from Spanish] Democratic Digitalisation, digital sovereignty for the people (Rayo Verde, 2024); Vote and get paid. Impunity as a form of government with Sergio Salgado (Capitán Swing, 2017); Technopolitics, internet and r-evolutions and Free digital culture – Basic notions to defend what belongs to everyone, (both Icaria Publishing, 2012). Creator of high-impact festivals, her plays have toured throughout Europe. We highlight Hazte Banquero, 2016-2017; Los OXcars, the largest free culture event of all time, 2008-2013; Advanced Realities, 2007-2009 / 2018-2019; Non lavoreremo mai, 2002-2005; and Femina ex Machina, 1999-2003.

Contents

Introduction 11

PART 1 - Disinformation History: None of This is an Internet Invention.. 15

    1. Propaganda. A brief history of fake news and information manipulation in the Global North.............. 17

    2. Follow the money. Deconstructing the foundational cases of contemporary disinformation.......................... 26

    An industrial-scale set-up, affordable only for a few............. 26

    Part 1 conclusion: anywhere, everywhere, anytime, every time 41

PART 2 - Current Approaches To Disinformation And Why They Do Not Work.. 45

1 - Biases in the definition of fake news and disinformation........ 47

    The definition of 'disinformation' as a diversionary manoeuvre.. 47

    Modalities of falsehoods and human nature........................ 52

    An action-oriented definition of 'disinformation'.................... 55

2 - Legislative moods that damage civil rights and freedoms... 56

    A case study: how European institutions deal with disinformation... 58

3. Fact-checking is not enough... 70

Codes of practice for journalism and fact-checkers - ABC of verification... 73

PART 3 - Let's Do The Right Thing.................................. 77

1. Preventive, compulsory labelling of institutional communication and (dis) information businesses.................. 79

Information, opinion, propaganda or advertising: who is who and what they do... 82

It is not about Truth; it is about the *duty of verification*....... 83

2 - Rules for dismantling the disinformation industry.............. 87

Following the money works................................... 89

Online and OFFLINE....................................... 96

Conclusion - To Combat Disinformation: More Democracy....... 100

Introduction

> I saw newspaper reports which did not bear any relation to the facts, not even the relationship which is implied in an ordinary lie. I saw great battles reported where there had been no fighting, and complete silence where hundreds of men had been killed. I saw troops who had fought bravely denounced as cowards and traitors, and others who had never seen a shot fired hailed as the heroes of imaginary victories, and I saw newspapers (...) retailing these lies and eager intellectuals building emotional superstructures over events that had never happened. I saw, in fact, history being written not in terms of what happened but of what ought to have happened accordingto various 'party lines'.
>
> - George Orwell,
> *Looking Back on the Spanish War* (1943)

Conferences about disinformation are mainstream. They are appealing, and institutions love them. They all seem to follow the same formula: a star speaker, boasting a fashionable biography (that omits the financial or client-affective ties to a political party) rattles off a list of stereotypical evils of technology, leading to a conclusion that could be summarised like this: "Given the very new danger of disinformation and fake news brought by the Internet and Artificial Intelligence (AI), for your own sake, the solution is to create institutions that ensure that internet and digital are not evil and - basically - 'regulate' freedom of expression in the digital era for the sake of the Truth."

This false conclusion is the main reason for this book: fake news is used as an excuse to curtail civil rights.

This book aims to serve as a tool to defend our freedoms and, at the same time, to act against new forms of manipulation and lying. It aims to dismantle the myths on which the new wave of freedom-crushing legislation rides, and to provide a new way of facing propaganda/disinformation.

The measures and the narrative that lay the groundwork for the policies around disinformation focus on Internet users and embrace a logic of control and censorship by either public or private players. These policies neglect subjects who generate and benefit from disinformation the most. In the following pages, we will demonstrate that all roads to the source of systemic disinformation lead to the same place: political parties, their structures of interest and influence, and the institutions they inhabit, which means other powerful, privileged stakeholders, from institutions to media to companies (in no particular order).

Fake news is far from a new phenomenon. It is also no novelty that those who hold the monopoly on manipulating information use manipulating information as an excuse to champion laws that curtail freedom of information and criminalise the use of new technologies, such as the Internet or AI, in this case.

The first thing that needs to be done to combat fake news is to avoid being fooled by the people who cause the problem. In other words, we must dismantle the narrative framework of propaganda surrounding the issue. In line with the distorted notion of disinformation presented to the public, the dominant private or public sectors are not obliged to change their long-standing propaganda methods. Instead, they only need to make new deals with their new competitors, the online content corporations. To perpetuate the asymmetry of power between them and the public, all they need to do is criminalise the technology itself and thus persecute democratic access to it by the public.

Throughout history, it has been not the general public but governments, institutions, political parties, mass media outlets, wealthy individuals and powerful corporations who have been primarily responsible for creating and disseminating disinformation that has altered the course of history. This is for a straightforward reason: they are the ones who can afford it. The fact that ordinary citizens play only an instrumental role in creating systemic lies is not because of any intrinsic moral superiority. To achieve real, massive reach in the creation of disinformation one needs resources, and ordinary people do not have them.

Given the lack of such resources, freedom of expression and access to information has proved to be the only viable instrument for uncovering the systemic and systematic lies forced on us by these large disinformation producers.

For these reasons, we need to reduce disinformation through having less technophobia and criminalisation of freedoms; less impunity and uninformed paternalism; less monopoly over the media and information resources; and more institutional accountability. In short, we need more and better democracy, plus an empowered public that monitors and watches what power says and does.

Recognising the complexity of the current context, the situation must not only be addressed in a way that respects freedom of expression and information but should be achieved using these freedoms. This means an increase in defence of the Internet and a shift from the current information monopolies towards a different model based on both the redignification of journalism as a profession, and democratic and distributed oversight of institutions in general, including their 'production' of information in particular.

New technologies allow first-degree verification mechanisms to be within everyone's reach. These mechanisms include fact-checking searches with AI or search engines, such as Google or any other that is more privacy-friendly. As never before, distributed verification is now a real possibility. It is a tool that democratises —at least in part— verification of the 'truth', something that until 30 years ago was in the hands of journalism, researchers, authorities and just a few more. If we wish to preserve fundamental freedoms, we cannot resign ourselves to accepting new gatekeepers who decide what is truth and what is a lie for everyone.

For this reason, we propose another strategy: follow the money.

Disinformation causes a massive impact when institutions and investments promote it, aiming to generate political, financial or other benefits. By focusing on profit, the behaviour of institutions, and the financial transactions surrounding the creation and circulation of information, we can avoid maiming freedom of expression—which is admittedly imperfect but can be practised for free—and deal with something that can be regulated: business.

With this approach, we propose a 'duty of verification' attached to institutions and / or payments made and received for emitting and viralising information. There are no oaths to truth; just the requirement to show how the information has been verified.

Initiatives that involve delegating the fight against disinformation to a select few, whether through a government body or a private company, cannot be enough since they carry a real risk of curtailing fundamental rights, suppressing critical voices and imposing pensée unique and propaganda. The fact that the Internet allows distributed access to verification is a good reason too for mandatory transparency (the traceability of sources) for the institutional producers of information or for the for-profit producers. Having procedures for this purpose is a deterrent to disinformation in itself.

So, let's see how we can get there.

PART 1

Disinformation History:
None of This is an Internet Invention

By the King.

A PROCLAMATION

To Restrain the Spreading of False News, and Licentious talking of Matters
OF

State and Government.

CHARLES R.

Whereas of late many persons ill affected to the Government have assumed to themselves a Liberty in their ordinary Discourses to censure and defame the Proceedings of State, whereby they endeavour to create and nourish in the minds of His Majesties good Subjects an ill opinion of things they understand not, And further to promote their Seditious ends, they do daily invent false News, and spread the same abroad amongst the People, to the great scandal of His Majesties Government: Whereof His Majesty taking notice, and in particular of that very false Report of an intention to dissolve this present Parliament, which hath not been under deliberation. His Majesty seeing no cause to change His resolutions taken touching their meeting: His Majesty therefore looks upon the Spreaders of that Report as persons Seditiously inclined and ill affected to His Service. And considering that by the Laws of this Realm great and heavy penalties are to be inflicted upon all such as shall be found to be Spreaders of false News, or promoters of any Malicious Calumnies against the State by their ordinary and common Discourses to stir up hatred in the People of His Majesties Person and the established Government, whereof His Majesty is sensible the persons offending are not ignorant. Nevertheless, that all men may be left without excuse who shall not hereafter contain themselves within that modest and dutiful regard which they ought, His Majesty hath thought fit, by the advice of His Council, to publish this His Royal Proclamation, And doth hereby forewarn and straightly Command all His Loving Subjects of what state or condition soever they be, from the highest to the Lowest, that they presume not henceforth by any Writing or Speaking to utter or publish any false News or Reports, or to intermeddle with the Affairs of State and Government, or with the persons of any of His Majesties Counsellors or Ministers, in their common and ordinary Discourses, as they will answer the contrary at their utmost perils. And Whereas all vile and irreverent speeches touching matters of this high nature are punishable not onely in the Speakers but the hearers also, unless they be speedily Reveal the same unto some of His Majesties Privy Council, or some other His Majesties Judges or Justices of the Peace: His Majesty doth hereby further Declare, that he will proceed with all severity not onely against such persons as shall utter any vile and unlawful speeches of this nature, but also against those persons who shall be present where such speeches are used, without Revealing the same in due time, His Majesty being resolved to Suppress this Unlawfull and Undutifull kind of Discourse, by a most strict and exemplary Punishment of all such Offenders as shall hereafter be Discovered.

Given at Our Court at Whitehall, the Second day of May, 1674, in the Six and twentieth year of Our Reign.

God save the King.

LONDON,
Printed by the Assigns of *John Bill* and *Christopher Barker*, Printers
to the Kings most Excellent Majesty. 1674.

1. Propaganda. Global North's brief history of fake news and information manipulation

A journey from the Neolithic period to the present day, to erase any lingering illusion that disinformation is a new Internet or AI phenomenon.

By Guillem Martínez

It is not too complicated: disinformation is propaganda. Propaganda is not advertising; it is propaganda. It is issued by the state —or by a group or entity able or willing to constitute itself as such —but, unlike violence, it is not a state monopoly. Speaking of violence, Chomsky[1] defines propaganda as violence exercised by the state in a democracy. This invites us to view propaganda as a method to achieve goals that, in the past, were realised not through propaganda but through violence. In short, it invites us to view propaganda as an everyday occurrence in democracy, even if, as a discipline, it dates back to pre-democratic periods— a paradox that shows the cruel and abusive nature of propaganda.

Propaganda, in one form or another, has nevertheless existed as long as the state has existed. We can trace the first iterations of propaganda back to the Neolithic period . In recent years, archaeological records suggest that its origins may date back as far as the Palaeolithic period[2]. In southern Turkey, one of the earliest examples of statehood and perhaps propaganda is the archaeological complex of Göbekli Tepe[3]. It consists of an as-yet incalculable number of circular temples in a style similar to Stonehenge. These circles are enormous and originally had roofs. Inside, we can see what could be the oldest image of a god, carved on gigantic slabs. It is estimated that each slab must have been

1. Herman, E.S. and Chomsky, N., (1988). *Manufacturing Consent. The Political Economy of the Mass Media*. New York: Pantheon Books.

2. Petersen, M. B., and Skaaning, S. E., (2010). *Ultimate Causes of State Formation: The Significance of Biogeography, Diffusion, and Neolithic Revolutions*. Historical Social Research, 35(3 (133)), 200–226 — Retrieved from <https://pure.au.dk/portal/en/publications/ultimate-causes-of-state-formation-the-significance-of-biogeograp>.

3. Schmidt, K., (2000). *First came the temple, then the city.* Preliminary report on the excavations at Göbekli Tepe and Gürcütepe 1995–1999. Paléorient. 26-1, pp. 45-54. DOI: https://doi.org/10.3406/paleo.2000.4697

carried by at least sixty people, fed without agriculture or livestock. How do you get that many people to work that hard and in such an organised way on a massive project? Historians assume they were bound and led by some kind of authority radiating some sort of religious worldview that encouraged such gratuitous work. This worldview, and the way it is structured, is undoubtedly a kind of propaganda. Perhaps the slabs form its first fossil.

Propaganda is, therefore, the broadcasting of *truth* —broadcasting the correct worldview. Correct as deemed by the broadcaster, who expects something from it. It is also, therefore, a refutation of 'lies' or worldviews held to be incorrect. How have the concepts of truth and lies been refined and developed throughout history? What follows is a brief overview of what this propaganda discipline has served. In other words, the imposition of 'truth'.

In the Classical period, lying was part of intelligence. Gods lie. The Greek god Zeus, for example, continuously lies to Hera to avoid having his infidelities come to light. He usually does so in a funny or at least witty way. In other words, attractively and positively. This was presumably the value of the lie in aristocratic Greece, which codified the political lie. The Trojan Horse was a deception that solved a war but also a political problem, bringing disunity and despair to the Achaeans.

With the arrival of democracy in Greek city-states, lies took on more sophisticated political forms, supported by language through the formulas of rhetoric. In Assembly Women, a comedy by the playwright Aristophanes, various formulae are presented for the real-time manipulation of an assembly of citizens by their leaders, based on language and the execution of public actions at the most effective moment.

This use of lies, rhetoric and manipulation of human groups may have been the norm —combined with the use of force, of course— in the forms of state up until Christianity, when propaganda gained a resource of unprecedented value: absolute truth[4]. Absolute truth in the political sphere presupposes the existence of states and monarchies in direct

---

4. (2001). *English Standard Version Bible*. ESV Online. Retrieved from <https://esv.literalword.com/>.

relation to God. It is God personified who establishes what truth and falsehood are. The earthly powers used this resource effectively once they discovered it was less cumbersome, inconvenient and expensive than force alone.

There is truth, and the state defends it. Whoever gets in the way of the truth or the state is the lie. The state also utilises other domination tools. Two things can strengthen it:

a) Beauty, or the prestige of art. The state demonstrates its power through art and public works, which are propaganda items. Florence and Rome, for example, are cities full of art. In other words, propaganda of the time. However, it also needs something new. It needs:

b) Reason, the use of arguments [5]. The humanist era saw the birth of a genre that would be the backbone of propaganda and counter-propaganda for centuries. Humanist dialogue, literary pieces —such as Diálogo de las cosas acaecidas en Roma, by Alfonso de Valdés[6] — in which various characters discuss a political act —in this case, the sacking of papal Rome by the troops of Charles— establishing who was right (in this case, the Emperor, not the Pope). This would have been a pretty unusual propaganda feat a few years earlier, when the Pope's propaganda resources, authority and ability to use it exceeded those of the state.

In the 18th century, propaganda gained in visuality. Yes, indeed, propaganda, in the past, had a significant visual element, perhaps the best in all of history: the cross. But then these elements were diversified (a factor that is both important and novel), gained depth, and took on a distinct political capacity. Benjamin Franklin (also an engraver, let us not forget) was, for example, the author of an extensive series of revolutionary illustrations, notably the famous snake., which was very

---

5. Gombrich E., H. (2006). *The Story of Art,* London: Phaidon Press, 978-0-7148-324-70.

6. Valdés, A. de. (2004). *Diálogo de las cosas acaecidas en Roma.* Alicante: Biblioteca Virtual Miguel de Cervantes. Retrieved from <http://www.cervantesvirtual.com/nd/ark:/59851/bmcq52j5>.

successful in the 13 colonies[7]. Apparently, it was usual to see it in the homes of pro-independence supporters. It was, therefore, a kind of pop art long before such a thing existed: an icon that was not religious but political and effective.

Soon after, the same thing happened in Europe. The French Revolution brought about political upheaval and, with it, an unprecedented change of mentality. Genres of propaganda such as dialogue remain today, where a single voice speaks to the reader ideologically; this was libel, a new genre. State propaganda also gained prominence through a new visual invention, which was to enjoy great fortune in the 19th and 20th centuries: the national flag. But also through new visual elements, such as a piece of jewellery, a brooch, graffiti or an image reproduced in series and hung on the wall of a house or a street.

In the 19th century, state propaganda was a baroque exercise. Propaganda was issued but not too necessary, as the state relied on force to solve the problems that it could have solved with it —problems with workers and nationalism, among others. The authoritarian state seriously resorted again to propaganda— massively and well, in an original way and, it seems from its results, effectively - in the foundational moment of the 20th century: the First World War[8,9]. States, allied powers and central powers faced the need to create large armies and maintain them without conceding rights (for example, the right to vote) to those citizens who were *invited* to become conscripts. This was a huge propaganda challenge and the result was epic. The central powers relied on the flag, the idea of Homeland as a value: on posters based on the flag, on national symbols, or on grievances inflicted by the enemy. The allied powers did so too, but they brought new features to the table, based on a new propaganda genre: the full-colour poster. In them, women were often shown being subjected to the barbarity of the opposing side, and the abuse and brutality of the enemy was invoked, against which people needed to defend themselves.

---

7. Kiger, P.J.. (28 September 2021). *How Ben Franklin's Viral Political Cartoon United the 13 Colonies*. History.com. Retrieved from <https://www.history.com/news/ben-franklin-join-or-die-cartoon-french-indian-war>.

8. *Propaganda in World War I*. (n.d.). in Wikipedia. Retrieved from <https://en.wikipedia.org/wiki/Propaganda_in_World_War_I#Use_of_patriotism_and_nationalism>.

9. *Propaganda*. (n.d.). in British Library. Retrieved from <https://support.bl.uk/Files/5b871ada-2ac9-42bf-bcbd-a07e00d39ffb/Propaganda-Exhibition-at-the-British-Library.pdf>.

State-modulated opinion- setting through posters reached its pinnacle in the United States. Woodrow Wilson, who stood for election on a promise not to go to war in Europe, came to power and immediately brought about a change in the country's collective[10] opinion using posters[11]. These basically invoked the brutality of the central armies against Serbian women. It is worth noting that the same theme was also extended to other media formats, such as cinema, for which small-scale propaganda films were produced, with German soldiers raping Serbian, French, and Polish women, or killing the children of these women after the abuse. The first propaganda films are still not too distant; perhaps one of them could be Tearing Down the Spanish Flag, from 1898[12], which depicts the American occupation of the island of Cuba. It shows, during its forty short seconds, how the Spanish flag is lowered and the American flag raised, supposedly in front of Morro Castle in Havana, although the video was actually shot on the rooftop of Vitagraph Studios in New York. Wilson's propaganda campaign raised the stakes and took things to a level never seen before. Thanks to that campaign, Wilson achieved something that until then had only been achieved through violence: forming a social majority in the process that resulted in, for example, voluntary enlisting in the army with conviction.

In the golden age of the poster, Soviet propaganda briefly took over from American propaganda. One might think that the greater the violence, the lesser the propaganda broadcast, or the lower the quality. However, as an example, the next propaganda milestone, capable of finding mechanisms of social communication and propaganda that continue to be studied and used in our time, came from a regime which relied absolutely on repression and crime, but which, despite this, cultivated, experimented with and studied propaganda with an intensity never seen before. This was Nazism.[13]

---

10. O'Toole, P. (21 October 2019). *When the U.S. Used 'Fake News' to Sell Americans on World War I.* History.com. Retrieved from <https://www.history.com/news/world-war-1-propaganda-woodrow-wilson-fake-news>.

11. Daly, C. B. (28 April 2014). *How Woodrow Wilson's propaganda machine changed American journalism.* The Conversation. Retrieved from <https://theconversation.com/how-woodrow-wilsons-propaganda-machine-changed-american-journalism-76270>.

12. Blackton, J.S and Smith, A.E., (1898). *Tearing Down the Spanish Flag* [FILM]. Vitagraph Company of America.

13. Martin, T. (2020). *Propaganda: How Germany Convinced the Masses.* History in

Goebbels, it seems, was no genius, but he was a brilliant philologist and, therefore, capable of studying and structuring effective discourse. His contributions to the discipline of propaganda are well known[14]. His first legislation was to unite all cultural fields in a compulsory association, as in the Soviet Union. Today, such unions are created through common sense, that is, through the bombardment of propaganda that shapes common sense[15]. The second contribution was radically new: the production of a popular, inexpensive radio[16]. This achieved the possibility of broadcasting propaganda into every household in the state. At the same time, he unified all radio stations and news programmes[17]. Good at learning from mistakes, Goebbels reformulated propaganda after the disaster of the Nazi defeat at Stalingrad, the beginning of the end. He made some significant little discoveries. For example, he realised that propaganda had to be fun. He discovered that the most effective way to disseminate it was not through news programmes or serious programmes but through frivolous programmes, even variety shows. This is the same type of programme in which propaganda is broadcast in today's democracies during the morning and evening television slots. He also discovered that cinema's propaganda cannot be only ideological but must broadcast structural propaganda only in certain sections or confuse it— which amounts to the same thing —with values interpreted as common sense and linked to nationalism, the main gateway to propaganda discourse. This is also the case, for example, in the US war and propaganda films of the time. Leisure films, with the occasional propaganda twist, depict German or Japanese characters as villains while the protagonists are good or innocent.

---

the Making: Vol. 13, Article 8. California State University, San Bernardino (CSUSB). Retrieved from <https://scholarworks.lib.csusb.edu/history-in-the-making/vol13/iss1/8/>.

14. Doob, L. W. (1950). *Goebbels' Principles of Propaganda*. The Public Opinion Quarterly, 14(3), 419–442. <https://www.jstor.org/stable/2745999>.

15. United States Holocaust Memorial Museum. (n.d.). *Culture in the Third Reich: Overview.* Holocaust Encyclopedia. Retrieved from <https://encyclopedia.ushmm.org/content/en/article/culture-in-the-third-reich-overview>.

16. Meier, A.C., (30 August 2018). *An Affordable Radio Brought Nazi Propaganda Home.* Jstor Daily. Retrieved from <https://daily.jstor.org/an-affordable-radio-brought-nazi-propaganda-home/>.

17. Marsh, A. (30 March 2021). *Inside the Third Reich's Radio Joseph Goebbels commissioned a stylish, mass-producible radio to channel Nazi propaganda into German homes.* IEEE Spectrum. Retrieved from <https://spectrum.ieee.org/inside-the-third-reichs-radio>.

Thankfully, Goebbels barely experimented with television. The Third Reich had few television receivers for only a short period, and he was wholly mistaken in his prediction of how this medium would develop. He predicted that watching would be collective, that no one would have an individual television set, but rather there would be a common television room in apartment buildings. However, he got one thing spot on: he thought that television reception should be modulated by a *weighted viewer*, i.e. a viewer with supremacy over the rest, who would comment on, evaluate and validate what the rest watched. This 'weighted viewer', by the way, would have the same function as that of the modern-day commentator, talk-show host or influencer.

In the 1930s and 1940s, in the wake of totalitarianism in Europe, the first electoral analysis was carried out in the United States[18]. The Democratic Party wanted to study whether radio as a propaganda system was indeed as important as its use during the Nazi upsurge seemed to suggest. It was discovered that it was not. Radio was important only because of the *weighted viewer*, that person who in his building, his place of work, his village, his neighbourhood, his peer group, had an influence on others and formed the backbone of opinion (as we will explain later on, via the concept of complex contagion). In short, it was discovered that information, even propaganda, had to be weighted by someone; It had to be highlighted by someone to be accepted more broadly across society[19].

The importance of propaganda mechanisms in democracy is so strikingly pronounced that there is a model[20] that catalogues propaganda strategies, how propaganda is used, in an everyday and undisciplined way, in democracy. These strategies are common in any democratic country, and are more intense now[21].

---

18. *Gallup, Inc.* (12 July 2006). in Wikipedia. Retrieved from <https://en.wikipedia.org/wiki/Gallup_(company)>.

19. Cantril, H. and Strunk, M. (1951). *Public opinion*, 1935-1946. Princeton: Princeton University Press. pp. 703-727. Retrieved from <https://archive.org/details/in.ernet.dli.2015.128827/page/n757/mode/2up?view=theater>.

20. Attributed to Chomsky, which actually seems to have been created by Sylvain Timsit. Timsit, S. (2002). *Stratégies de manipulation*. [Manupulation strategies]. Retrieved from <http://www.syti.net/Manipulations.html>.

21. The strategies are as follows:

Another set of descriptions of and responses to the everyday use of propaganda can be found in cognitive linguistics, which describes propaganda in terms of linguistic-neural processes. This school of thought has discovered that reality is not as important as the perception of reality, and that perception modulates the experience of reality through mental biases that are easily manipulated. By applying these theories to the study of propaganda, it has been discovered that ideology is created and transmitted through one of the most simple, spectacular, brilliant, every day and amusing rhetorical devices: the metaphor[22]. The use of metaphors makes mental frameworks[23] that, in turn, generate neural circuits or pathways. When they have been created in a person's head, using that pathway then generates pleasure. Neural pathways supplant reasonable analysis —or worse, they are the only reasonable analysis we have access to in the first instance— meaning they continue to exist and are used even once reality has shown that the framework was either a lie or incorrect [24].

• Distraction: diverting attention away from important, structural problems.

• Create problems, then offer solutions: the state's ability to create urgent agendas for problems that it chooses to consider important; problems to which the state presents solutions, thus managing to showcase its performance as a political achievement.

• Gradual: the strategy of not taking measures that are unacceptable to society directly, but rather introducing them gradually.

• Defer: label a measure as painful and necessary, pretending not to be in favour of it, so that the public gets used to the idea of change and accepts it with resignation when the time comes.

• Speak down to the public: treat the public, i.e. the recipients of propaganda, like children. Commonly through language that is infantile.

• Appeal to people's emotions: arouse the public's emotions rather than inviting reflection.

• Keep people in the dark: use complicated terms —economic, for example— to avoid information and transparency.

• Normalisation of mediocrity: normalise the linguistic and intellectual categories of politicians.

• Reinforce self-blame: make people believe that they are solely responsible for their misfortunes, because of their low level of intelligence, poor skills or an inability to try hard enough.

• Data elision: know individuals better than they know themselves. In recent decades there has been a major development in the scientific knowledge (biology, neurobiology and applied psychology) of ordinary citizens and the elites are able to accurately anticipate the public's behavioural patterns.

22. Underhill, J.W. (2011). *Creating worldviews: Metaphor, ideology and language*. New York: Edinburgh University Press. ISBN 9780748643158.

23. Boroditsky, L. (2011) *Metaphors we think with: the role of metaphor in reasoning.*

24. Curtis, A. (2015). *The Century of the Self- Happiness Machine*. [VIDEO].

Without a doubt, the new propaganda frameworks are aware of the contributions made by cognitive linguistics, and use them to construct post-truth. Fake news does not mean lies. Or rather, they are not just lies. It is not the Trojan horse that we mentioned at the start of this chapter, but rather it is proof that the Trojan horse was indeed a gift from the gods, as the Trojans thought. Proof even that it was not a horse, perhaps, or that there was no horse. Fake news creates reality and creates perceptions of reality. It creates these perceptions by adding sentimental and, by extension, unverifiable values and components to a given news item. It creates sentimentality and, through that, metaphors; through metaphors, it creates frameworks; through frameworks, it creates neural pathways. The result is a reality based on sentimental values, which propaganda can modulate ideologically. Sentimentality affects the creation of identities, which are then susceptible to feeling aggrieved. Fake news and post-truth confirm identity-based grievances. For example, a white, heterosexual father and husband can find grievance in the idea that he does not exist as a recognised and promoted identity, and as a result, he feels constantly attacked, causing him to mobilise politically in one direction and not in another. It is important to keep in mind that this politicisation of identity, which both responds to tension and causes tension in turn, is realised through suffering. Personal suffering, the way we perceive it, the way it grows, the way it is manipulated, is at the epicentre of a breeding ground for propaganda.

[Adding by Simona Levi: partisan politics is not there to solve suffering; it lives out of it.]

2. Follow the money — Deconstructing the foundational cases of contemporary disinformation

Investing in the disinformation business: press, mining of personal data, bots, cyborgs, echo chambers, artificial intelligence and noise in the networks.

An industrial-scale set-up affordable only for a few

So, how is disinformation distributed and created nowadays? Who creates and pays for fake news, and who receives payment for creating and making it go viral?

Those financing disinformation, which can be referred to as the producers of disinformation in what is a full-blown industry, include governments, institutions and political parties (at times acting as producers of disinformation, at others as investors so that another actor can create and viralise it), shareholders and directors of mass media outlets, large corporations, individuals with significant fortunes and celebrities. Those who are paid to create tailor-made fake news or viralise it include communications companies, political communication consultants, companies specialising in algorithmic governance, media outlets and online content platforms. We can call these actors high-impact information producers because of their extensive reach among the population. If the fake news phenomenon is really to be tackled, these actors -the producers of disinformation and those who pay and receive payment to spread it- should be our main targets.

It is difficult, therefore, to imagine how those who have the power to enforce policies can put an end to the problem: they are the same people who pay and benefit from it.

Let's look again from this 'follow the money' approach at some of the historic and best-known cases of systemic disinformation. We can then understand how the industrial process of creating and disseminating fake news - the actual fake news, the news that undermines democracy - acts. As described in the previous chapter, the techniques and formats involved may evolve over time, with differing technologies, but the interests and objectives remain the same.

In the Steve Bannon school, in Donald Trump's and new far-right methodology[25], we have seen since the beginning a massive use of personalised propaganda for a segmented target population.

The current boom of the narrative on the fake news phenomenon in the media started in the 2016 US presidential election[26]. Donald Trump himself, the winner of that election, popularised the term. His campaign exacerbated the showmanship of politics and relied on polarisation as content in and of itself. Following, in particular, the methodology of Bannon, his former chief strategist trained with extremist outlets in increasing impact, fake news was fabricated without any pretence, shame or denial. It was created to an exponentially higher degree than usual, and in a way that is now the style of many parties.

Once the winner was proclaimed, the Cambridge Analytica and Facebook scandal erupted. Cambridge Analytica worker Christopher Wylie revealed to The Observer and The Guardian that millions of users' data were extracted from the social network without their knowledge or permission and sold for targeting pro-Trump propaganda[27]. The political and legal fallout from the scandal made headlines. Still, Managing Director Mark Zuckerberg only implemented measures to prevent a repeat of the scandal when a campaign called for the public to quit his platform[28].

Several studies have attempted to analyse the impact fake news had on the outcome of those elections. The ability of such propaganda to use personal data to fine-tune a message according to who receives it to change opinion, as well as voting intentions, appears to be highly effective. It provides not merely a generic slogan broadcast across

25. Tucker Carlson (8 July 2004). in *Wikipedia.* Retrieved from <https://en.wikipedia.org/wiki/Tucker_Carlson>.

26. Drobnic Holan, A. (13 December 2016). *2016 Lie of the Year: Fake news.* PolitiFact. Retrieved from <https://www.politifact.com/article/2016/dec/13/2016-lie-year-fake-news/>.

27. Cadwalladr, C. (18 March 2018). *I made Steve Bannon's psychological warfare tool: meet the data war whistleblower.* The Guardian. Retrieved from <https://www.theguardian.com/news/2018/mar/17/data-war-whistleblower-christopher-wylie-faceook-nix-bannon-trump>.

28. Newton, C. (22 March 2018). *Facebook's Cambridge Analytica data scandal, explained* [VIDEO]. The Verge. Retrieved from <https://www.youtube.com/watch?v=VDR8qG-myEQg>.

various media outlets but a personalised message that hits every target right in the centre[30,31,32,33,34] and creates *filterbubbles*[35]. The fact that the public lives in an information bubble is not new. Humans have always preferred to see what they want, not what is necessarily there.

Moreover, the channels for information dissemination have always belonged to monopolistic actors, be they governments or companies, with their own information biases. Ownership of mass media conditions the conceptual framework, with narratives constructed according to the interests of economic elites and governments. The journalistic profession has notorious difficulty maintaining its independence... "

Other factors are now coming into play. For better or worse, the Internet has weakened the media, which was until recently the sole intermediary between information and information consumers. As with the advent of writing and the printing press, the advent of the Internet has, on the one hand, led to disintermediation, allowing for the democratisation of access to and generation of information. On the other hand, it has opened the door to a reconfiguration of intermediation and has made possible other forms of information bubbles, such as online platforms. What sets apart the current situation is that biases can be predictively generated and automatically configured.

---

29. Pariser, E. (March 2011). *Beware of online filterbubbles* [VIDEO]. TED Conferences, LLC. Retrieved from <https://www.ted.com/talks/eli_pariser_beware_online_filter_bubbles/up-next>.

30. Gunther, R., Beck, P. A., and Nisbet, E. C. (2018). *Fake News May Have Contributed to Trump's 2016 Victory*. Ohio State University. Retrieved from <https://www.documentcloud.org/documents/4429952-Fake-News-May-Have-Contributed-to-Trump-s-2016.html>.

31. Blake, A. (3 April 2018). *A new study suggests fake news might have won Donald Trump the 2016 election*. The Washington Post. Retrieved from <https://www.washingtonpost.com/news/the-fix/wp/2018/04/03/a-new-study-suggests-fake-news-might-have-won-donald-trump-the-2016-election/>.

32. Marchal, N., Neudert, L. M., Kollanyi, B., and Howard, P. N. (2018). *Polarization, Partisanship and Junk News Consumption on Social Media During the 2018 US Midterm Elections*. Data Memo 2018.5. Oxford, UK: Project on Computational Propaganda. University of Oxford. Retrieved from <https://demtech.oii.ox.ac.uk/research/posts/polarization-partisanship-and-junk-news-consumption-on-social-media-during-the-2018-us-midterm-elections/#continue>.

33. Summary of interviews originally published on Furtherfield.com: Decarli, L. (3 July 2018). *Review of the HATE NEWS CONFERENCE* by Disruption Network Lab.

34. Pariser, E. (March 2011). *Beware of online "filter bubbles* [VIDEO]. TED

The algorithms of Facebook, Twitter, Google, Amazon and others discriminate information without consulting us while they promote the fallacy that we navigate freely[35]. We are never clearly told that this is not the case, that the algorithms of these companies create a unique universe for each individual user, exacerbating the ideological and emotional tendencies that the algorithm ascribes to us based on our age, location, taste etc. This causes the algorithm to suggest very different choices for each person, using behavioural addiction techniques to favour clients who are not the users but rather the advertisers, with the only goal of increasing the time users spend on the service via the more commented and controversial content[36]. This was (and is) already the case with conventional media; in social networks, this happens in an even more capillary and precise way[37] and it breaks one of the principles that make the Internet a tool for democratisation: it breaks neutrality. So, please, let's not blame the Internet; let's blame the power and the corporations that have occupied it.

Although they are three distinct phenomena, polarisation, bubble filters, and the spread of fake news go hand in hand and feed one another. All three respond to the classic phases of mass control -divide, isolate, manipulate- and do not represent anything new. Neither can they be considered dynamics *native* to the digital age.

Polarisation is accompanied by echo chambers[38]: people with a particular opinion end up interacting only with other people and content that share their own position, in a feedback loop that reinforces the perceived popularity of one's own opinion. The most obvious case is communication by political parties, especially during election campaigns:

Conferences, LLC. Retrieved from <https://www.ted.com/talks/eli_pariser_beware_online_filter_bubbles/up-next>.

35. Allcott, Hunt, et al. (2024). The effects of Facebook and Instagram on the 2020 election: A deactivation experiment. Proceedings of the National Academy of Sciences, 121(21), e2321584121. Retrieved from <https://www.pnas.org/doi/10.1073/pnas.2321584121>.

36. Leanizbarrutia, I. (20 February 2019). *Twitter, esa caverna de Platyn 2.0.*

37. Lanier, J. (2018). *Ten Arguments for Deleting your Social Media Accounts Right Now.* London, United Kingdom: Bodley Head Limited. ISBN 1847925391 (ISBN13: 9781847925398).

38. *Echo chamber* (media). (n.d.). in Wikipedia. Retrieved from <https://en.wikipedia.org/wiki/Echo_chamber_(media)>.

it generates very clear echo chambers inhabited by sympathisers of the same party or political-ideological space.

They are the combined effect of human psychological dispositions and the action of filter bubbles[39]. Mathematical models link the diffusion of a given piece of information to the existence of echo chambers. This iteration of the information diffusion model, called complex contagion[40], is a classic in which each social actor, each individual, is embedded in a network of contacts.

The individuals or groups with whom we interact socially can be referred to as our *neighbours*. Each of us has an *activation threshold*: if the fraction of its neighbours disseminating information exceeds this threshold, the actor will be convinced and start sharing the information themselves.

The activation threshold may depend on the specific nature of the piece of information and the type ofcontact network. For example, when individuals within an echo chamber have a low activation threshold in relation to other actors in that chamber, computer simulations show that information spreads quicker and more profoundly when the contact network has a certain degree of polarisation against external actors[41].

In short, current massive echo chambers are the same as previous ones: they are created by communication departments crafting political or corporate messages.The tools are better, that's true: algorithms for personalising messaging, AI to improve it, and online social platforms exploiting and amplifying certain human cognitive attitudes.

---

39. Pariser, E. (2011). *The Filter Bubble: What the Internet is Hiding from You.* New York: Penguin Group. 294 pp. ISBN: 978-0-670-92038-9.

40. *Complex contagion.* (n.d.). in Wikipedia. Retrieved from <https://en.wikipedia.org/wiki/Complex_contagion>.
Spohr, D. (2017). *Fake news and ideological polarization.* Business Information Review,34(3),150–160.doi:10.1177/0266382117722446 (https://www.ethicaldigital.ca/blog/fake-news-and-ideological-polarization)
Schmidt, A. L., Zollo, F., Scala, A., Betsch, C., and Quattrocioc- chi, W. (2018). *Polarization of the vaccination debate on Facebook.* Vaccine, 36(25), 3606-3612.
Pariser, E. (2011). *The Filter Bubble: What the Internet is Hiding from You.* New York: Penguin Group.
Weaver, Iain S. et al. (2019). *Communities of online news expo- sure during the UK General Election 2015.* Online Social Networks and Media. 10-11:18-30.

41. Emanuele Cozzo y Luce Prignano.

The tools are better, but the intention and authors haven't changed an inch.

Fake news reinforces a person's level of identification with the group whose worldview they share. The information confirms this, cementing the echo chambereffect in a feedback loop that is difficult to break. Once the mechanism is understood, any interested actor can leverage it to create favourable conditions for disseminating a given narrative[42].

In the system used by Bannon[43], the 'Leni Riefenstahl of the Tea Party movement'[44]—now very common in political communication society into hermetic ideological and cultural ghettos with different worldviews, and then reconstructing it according to one's vision to achieve cultural hegemony.

Deep Fake: The "gothic" cathedral of Barcelona, visited every year by 32 millions tourists. In fact, this faзade was built in 1913 so, I'm sorry, it is not Gothic. It's a deep fake we cannot blame on AI.

To do so, one must exploit the mechanisms of filter bubbles and deploy data-driven propaganda that tells everyone what they want to hear. In many events, like the Capitol attack in 2021, we see the same patterns in creating previously favourable public opinion[45].

---

42. Emanuele Cozzo y Luce Prignano.

43. *With All Due Respect. (*2016). How Seinfeld Explains Stephen Bannon. Retrieved from <https://www.bloomberg.com/news/videos/2016-08-17/how-seinfeld-explains-stephen-bannon>.

44. *Bloomberg. (*2015). *Steve Bannon: This Man Is the Most Dangerous Political Operative in America.* Retrieved from <https://www.bloomberg.com/politics/graphics/2015-steve-bannon/>.

45. Robertson, L. (6 January 2022.) FactChecking Claims About the Jan. 6 Capitol Riot. *FactCheck.org.* Retrieved from <https://www.factcheck.org/>.
Silverman, C. et al. (4 January 2022). Facebook groups topped 10,000 daily attacks on

Here, as in other areas, we can see that it would not be too complicated to introduce legislation that would apply to institutions and the (dis) information industry meant to enforce previous verification and transparency. This legislation would ensure that institutions and the (dis) information business could not with impunity use AI and algorithms that do not respect civil rights and the privacy of individuals. For this to be possible, we need the tracking and the recommendation algorithms and protocols to be regulated and auditable; users should have control. In this respect there are many civil society organisations that are working to stop the use of algorithmic manipulation. Organisations such as AI Forensics[46], which investigates influential and opaque algorithms to uncover and expose the harms caused by their producers, or Noyb, which is proving that OpenAI could correct wrong information[47]. Most of us are members of the coalition PeopleVSBigTech[48].

Let us now look at the media. First, we want to say it out loud: there is still good journalism: investigative, reliable journalism, indispensable journalism.

That said, what is going on with the sector? It is worth mentioning[49] that in the 1980s a business management model, the Rupert Murdoch model, which consisted of turning journalism into just another business dedicated mainly to recycling information to reduce costs, arrived. On top of that, media outlets now have to compete for advertising revenues with the online advertising and platform giants, adding to previous biases brought about by the new advertising market[50]. And now, we

---

election before Jan. 6. *Washinhton Post*. Retrieved from <https://www.washingtonpost.com/technology/2022/01/04/facebook-election-misinformation-capitol-riot/>.
Stuart, A. (4 January 2022). Election Falsehoods Surged on Podcasts Before Capitol Riots, Researchers Find. *The New York Times*. Retrieved from <https://mediawell.ssrc.org/news-items/election-falsehoods-surged-on-podcasts-before-capitol-riots-researchers-find-the-new-york-times/>.

46. AIForensics. (n. d.). Retrieved from <https://aiforensics.org/>.

47. Noyb - European Center for Digital Rights. (29 April 2024.) *Complaint against OpenAI*. Retrieved from <https://noyb.eu/sites/default/files/2024-04/OpenAI%20Complaint_EN_redacted.pdf>.

48. People vs. Big Tech. (s. f.). Retrieved from <https://peoplevsbig.tech/>.

49. Davies, N. (2008). *Flat Earth News: An Awardwinning Reporter Exposes Falsehood, Distortion and Propaganda in the Global Media*. London, United Kingdom: Random House UK. ISBN 0701181451 (ISBN13: 9780701181451).

50. Tauber, A. (2023). Saving the news from Big Tech. *EUobserver*. Retrieved from

see a variable becoming increasingly amplified: political interference, through the financing of the media with institutional advertising. Due to the loss of advertising revenues because of competition in the digital arena, the vulnerability of the media has increased its dependence on different parties. There is a severe and non-democratic concentration of ownership of the mainstream media[51],[52].

The existence of apparently more diverse and pluralistic media offerings does not necessarily mean that this is actually the case. It is quite normal for a single media conglomerate to have both a left-wing and a right-wing TV channel to cover all audiences, enclosing them in either a left wing or a right-wing bubble and then providing both with the same advertisements and political propaganda tailored to their tastes[53],[54].

The outlook is even more serious if we take into account the fact that, following the financial crisis, the media concentrated into the hands of large financial conglomerates —mainly the banks, corporations or high-wealth individuals to which they owed money— and have, therefore lost all independence in some systemic fields, such as the financial system.

The journalistic code of ethics[55] is merely a guideline and not an obligation. Several media outlets have increasingly seen that fabricating information is more profitable than actual investigation or reporting. We have seen a proliferation of headlines created ad hoc, which, under the guise of media, are little more than channels of propaganda for the fabrication of biased news that may or may not be based on news

---

<https://euobserver.com/opinion/157187>.

51. Lutz, A. (24 June 2012). These 6 Corporations Control 90% of the Media in America. *Business insider.* Retrieved from <https://www.businessinsider.com/these-6-corporations-control-90-of-the-media-in-america-2012-6>.

52. Confessore, N. (4 April 2018).Cambridge Analytica and Facebook: The Scandal and the Fallout So Far. *The New York Times.* Retrieved from <https://www.aljazeera.com/news/2018/3/28/cambridge-analytica-and-facebook-the-scandal-so-far>.

53. Hern, A. (22 May 2017). How social media filter bubbles and algorithms influence the election. *The Guardian.* Retrieved from <https://www.theguardian.com/technology/2017/may/22/social-media-election-facebook-filter-bubbles>.

54. Newcombe, J. (24 June 2018). Fake News: Propaganda in the 21st Century. *Medium.* Retrieved from <https://medium.com/@jeremynewcombe_5950/fake-news-propaganda-in-the-21st-century-da13fdcd7ff5>.

55. For instance: Society of Professional Journalists. (2014). Code of Ethics. Retrieved from <https://www.spj.org/ethicscode.asp>.

items.

This shift only accentuates the tendency for many media outlets to engage in unverified replication of information passed down by governments and political parties as if they were reliable. In this context, the good independent media struggle. It is not uncommon to find information published in the mass media that has not even undergone a simple verification exercise available to anyone in the digital age, such as a search on a search engine. Can the so-called "democracies" afford to have the media outlets ecosystem —the so-called *public watchdogs*[56]—left in this situation?

In the context of wartime censorship, Marc Bloch, a historian, soldier and member of the French resistance killed by the Gestapo in 1944, saw the spread of fake news during the war. He reached the conclusion that when people can no longer trust the media, because they know that it serves interests other than the truth, society as a whole looks for other sources of information. This is obvious, he said, but is not the only needed condition: a fake news story cannot spread unless there is already a favourable context or collective thinking in place. Stereotypes are a shelter in uncertain times. However, "while methodical doubt is a sign of good mental health, excessive scepticism [note of Simona Levi: conspiratorial tendencies] is nothing more than a form of gullibility"[57].

As Whitney Phillips explains at length in *The Oxygen of Amplification*[58], even the media outlets that focus on fake news to explain that it is fake —be it out of genuine interest or to increase their audience because of the lurid nature of the news in question —are contributing to the spread of such fake information.

The Bannon —Trump school of thought bases its success on this, not least because it is cheaper: they produce highly provocative, aggressive and stereotypical hoaxes and then sit back and watch as their political

56. European Court of Human Rights. (8 November 2016). *In the case of Magyar Helsinki Bizottság v. Hungary*. Retrieved from <https://hudoc.echr.coe.int/eng#{%22ite-mid%22:[%22002-11282%22]}>.

57. Bloch, M. (1921). *Réflexions d'un historien sur les fausses nouvelles de la guerre*. Revue de synthèse historique, t.33, p. 13-35.

58. Phillips, W. (22 May 2018). The Oxygen of Amplification: Better Practices for Reporting on Extremists, Antagonists, and Manipulators Online. *Data & Society*. Retrieved from <https://datasociety.net/library/oxygen-of-amplification/>.

adversaries make them viral over and over again on social media, in opinion columns, in news stories, all the while screaming indignation and outrage, that sells so well.

The result is always the same: the problem lies not in the Internet but in the ideological or economic interests that are investors. The Internet is often merely just one of several spheres for dissemination.

Here is another example identifying the most significant producers of disinformation: since 2012 Alberto Escorcia, a Mexican Internet journalist and activist, has pioneered speaking out and identifying a new style of government-funded disinformation industry[59]. In his work, he documented the existence of armies of bots —computer programs that carried out automated tasks on social networks, replacing and mimicking human behaviour— artificially directing the conversation on the Internet and financed, during his mandate, by President Peña's entourage. He labelled them *Pecabots*[60]. Escorcia has had to remain in exile for several years due to death threats[61] as a result of his investigation while the disinformation industry in Mexico continues to operate.

More recently, armies of cyborgs who are human account operators, making detection increasingly difficult, replaced bots. Marta Peirano describes this phenomenon:

> Troll farms are a kind of call centre where hundreds of people create, manage and monitor hundreds of thousands of cyborg accounts. They are not hackers, because they don't need to be. They are unemployed advertisers, journalists, and salespeople, as well as students and struggling housewives. They don't need to be programmers; they just need to be familiar with social networks and be able to manage a swarm of cyborgs on various missions. Their salary depends on their efficiency, but they are not paid much. They are gig workers in a brutal economy.

59. Finley, K. (23 August 2015). Pro-Government Twitter Bots Try to Hush Mexican Activists. *Wired*. Retrieved from <https://www.wired.com/2015/08/pro-government-twitter-bots-try-hush-mexican-activists/>.

60. Soloff, A. K. (9 March 2017). Mexico's Troll Bots Are Threatening the Lives of Activists. *vice*. https://www.vice.com/en/article/mg4b38/mexicos-troll-bots-are-threatening-the-lives-of-activists

61. Redacción. (9 July 2016). Barcelona muestra su apoyo al activista mexicano amenazado Alberto Escorcia. *La Vanguardia*. Retrieved from <https://www.lavanguardia.com/politica/20160709/403075511555/barcelona-muestra-su-apoyo-al-activista-mexicano-amenazado-alberto-escorcia.html>

> Their job is to generate interest in new products -where cyborgs give positive reviews in forums, news items, or online shops- or to discredit competing products. Of course, they also apply when the 'product' is political. The companies that carry out these tactics are not always hired directly by the party but by "(...) the agency or spin doctor running the campaign" and are combined "(...) with aggressive Big Data and personalised marketing tools and platform profiling[62].

AI has improved content and efficiency. There is enough money to innovate and mutate, and innovation in this area is far from stagnant.

Bot or cyborgs can wear down dissent through constant personal attacks, exaggerate recipients' fears and anger by repeating short slogans, exaggerate popularity, derail conversations, distract attention to irrelevant, meaningless issues, and spread true or false news items on a large scale. Finding bot followers on very active, high-profile accounts is also widespread without the account owner knowing it. By following them, they hope to lend an air of credibility to the trend being reinforced by the bots. The mentions and trending topics created for the high-speed propagation of any given message or actor are vehicles for agendas and manipulation of the information being disseminated, including disinformation.

When someone benefits from disseminating a manipulated message, there are also those who can make money out of it. Finding companies that directly and openly offer followers for sale is easy. Buying a million Twitter followers ranges from 3,500 to 15,000 euros depending on language and other features.

As a result of field research by some analysts, such as Alberto Escorcia[63], an important fact can be observed: the great explosion of companies that offer this type of tool has been spurred on by celebrities eager for followers, wishing to appear more popular, or to interact with fans or detractors, without actually having to interact with them. Political

---

62. Peirano, M. (20 November 2017). No son bots rusos, es Capitalismo 3.0 reventando el debate político online. *eldiario.es*. Retrieved from <https://www.eldiario.es/politica/bots-rusos-cyborgs-mercena-%20rios_0_708680008.html>.

63. Escorcia, A. (2023). *Memorias de la guerra digital. . . y lo que viene*. Hotmart. Retrieved from <https://hotmart.com/es/marketplace/productos/memorias-de-la-guerra-digital-y-lo-que-viene/T84929235N>.

parties and governments are *clients* who have come to this industry at a later stage, but they are now as good as celebrities and looking for the same results[64,65,66]. Investing in advertising and commercial promotion for a political campaign, with T-shirts, mugs and the like, is twenty times more expensive than buying a basic online promotion and social media service[67].

AI, bots and cyborgs are a means, not the source of the problem. The problem is

> prominent figures and established organisations, not robots, that guide discussions. AI can be used to manipulate information; (Ro) bots can amplify a message. They do not by themselves create or change trends. Those responsible are, therefore, the ones who hire the service companies specialised in context and information manipulation[69].

Follow the money. This is precisely because it would be a relatively easy task to find out who pays for such professional services if legislators chose to do so.

That is why regulation is so important: we need to know the AI protocols and algorithms that govern us and influence public affairs. And we need fundamental rights and freedoms to be respected in programming to avoid dangerous biases.

Brazil has the second-highest WhatsApp usage in the world, after India[69]. 92% of the mobile phone-using population, or 68% of adults,

---

64. All, R. (2019). #112 The Prophet. Gimlet. https://gimletmedia.com/shows/reply-all/j4hl36

65. Barragán, A. (29 June 2018). Así se escriben las *fake news* durante la campaña electoral en México. *El País-Verne*. Retrieved from <https://verne.elpais.com/verne/2018/06/27/mexico/1530112534_124044.html>.

66. BuzzFeed News. (2018). *Meet Mexico's Fake News King*. Youtube. Retrieved from <https://youtu.be/ZZrCeAsjRUl>.

67. Fregoso, J. (2018). *#Mexico2018. Fake News and Social Media: The New Heads of the Hydra at University of Oxford*. University of Oxford. Retrieved from <https://reutersinstitute.politics.ox.ac.uk/our-research/mexico2018fake- news-and-social-media-new-heads-hydra>.

68. Vosoughi, S., Roy, D., y Aral, S. (2018), *op.* cit.

69. Dean, B. (2023). *WhatsApp User Statistics 2024: How many people use WhatsApp?*. Backlinko. Retrieved from <https://backlinko.com/whatsapp-users#top-10-

communicate using this messaging application[70].

Phone companies in many Latin American countries offer specific mobile data plans for WhatsApp. Starting from over eight dollars, users can sign up for plans with free, unlimited connection to the messaging application[71]. This undermines net neutrality, which is, in principle, guaranteed by the countries' legislation. Moreover, because chat lists are closed ecosystems, they are virtually impervious to refutation and fact-checking.

It is not surprising, then, that the disinformation and fake news industry made use of this messaging service during the election campaign that saw Bolsonaro win in 2018, in a context where mass media was heavily discredited. Bolsonaro was not represented in traditional media due to campaign quotas and did not give interviews. Nor did he participate in the election debates. His campaign was conducted mainly through social media and his appearances took place on his official accounts[72].

---

whatsapp-countries-by-audience>.
Gwi. (n. d.). *Social Media Trends: 2024 Global Report.* Retrieved from <https://www.gwi. com/reports/social>.

70. Exame 2016. (30 June 2016). Brasil é um dos países que mais usam Whats App, diz pesquisa.
Mensageria no Brasil – Fevereiro de 2020. (2021). Panorama Mobile Time/Opinion Box. Retrieved from <https://www.mobiletime.com.br/pesquisas/mensageria-no-brasil-fevereiro-de-2020/>.
De Souza, R.(2020). 95% dos brasileiros que usam o WhatsApp abrem o app todos os dias. Canaltech. Retrieved from <https://canaltech.com.br/apps/95-porcento-dos-brasileiros-que-usam-o-whatsapp-abrem-o-app-todos-os-dias-171055/>.
cetic.br. (29 August 2023). *Pesquisa sobre o uso das Tecnologias de Informa3ro e Comunica3ro nos domicílios brasileiros - TIC Domicílios 2022.* Retrieved from <https://cetic.br/pt/pesquisa/domicilios/publicacoes/>.
cetic.br. (25 November 2021). *Resumo Executivo — Pesquisa sobre o uso das Tecnologias de Informa3ro e Comunicaçro nos domicHlios brasileiros— TIC DomicHlios 2020.* Retrieved from <https://www.nic.br/publicacao/resumo-executivo-pesquisa-sobre-o-uso-das-tecnologias-de-informacao-e-comunicacao-nos-domicilios-brasileiros-tic-domicilios-2020/>.

71. Oliveira, J., y Rossi, M. (7 October 2018). WhatsApp, el elemento distorsionador de la campaña en Brasil. *El País.* Retrieved from <https://elpais.com/internacional/2018/10/07/america/1538877922_089599.html>.

72. Tejero, L. 2018. (30 October 2018.) Siete claves para entender el triunfo de Jair Bolsonaro en Brasil. *El Mundo.* Retrieved from <https://www.elmundo.es/internacional/2018/10/29/5bd723ace2704e40738b4667.html>.

The information was massively distributed via WhatsApp, through groups allegedly administered by supporters and volunteers who denied receiving any money in return, which was true in some cases[73]. They claimed they were doing so to combat lies about Bolsonaro in the mainstream media. Many of the messages spread via WhatsApp referenced the Bible (seven out of ten Brazilian evangelicals went on to vote for Bolsonaro), morality, child protection or spoke up against abortion and sexual freedoms and stoked conspiracy theories.[74,75,76,77]

Finally, the Brazilian newspaper Folha de S. Paulo reported that certain large companies financed the WhatsApp mass mailing in favour of Bolsonaro with three million dollars. The articles included proof of payments and other documents corroborating these connections. This practice is illegal under Brazilian law.[78,79]

Once again, we come to the same conclusion: when we talk about major disinformation producers, we must look first and foremost at the interests of political parties. In this case, large fortunes indirectly *donated* to parties by paying for massive disinformation campaigns in the traditional press and on the Internet.

In the Philippines, supporters of President Rodrigo Duterte use groupscalled *call centre hubs* to spread false and harmful information, including memes, and to target and har-ass those who are critical of the

---

73. Benites, A. 2018. (28 September 2018.) Nossos grupos combatem as notícias maldosas para desconstruir Bolsonaro. *El País*. Retrieved from <https://brasil.elpais.com/brasil/2018/09/26/politica/1537998612_052780.html>.

74. Gosálvez, P., Ser, G. del, Oliveira, J., Blanco, P., Hernández, F., Fernández, A., y Lin, L. (n. d.). Los 'whatsapps' de una campaña envenenada. *El País*. Retrieved from <https://elpais.com/especiales/2018/elecciones-brasil/conversaciones-whatsapp/>.

75. Marés, C., and Becker, C. (2018). *Sy 4 das 50 imagens mais compartilhadas por 347 grupos de WhatsApp são verdadeiras.*

76. Tardáguila, C., Benevenuto, F., and Ortellado, (17 October 2018.) Fake News Is Poisoning Brazilian Politics. WhatsApp Can Stop It. *New York Times.*

77. SUPERIOR ELECTORAL COURT (TSE). Memorandum of Understanding (MoU) between Whatsapp and TSE. (2020). Retrieved from < https://www.justicaeleitoral.jus.br/parcerias-digitais-eleicoes/assets/arquivos/memorando_whatsapp.pdf>.

78. Campos, P. 2018.(7 October 2018.) *Empresários bancam campanha contra o PT pelo WhatsApp*, Folha de S. Paulo.

79. Gutiérrez, B. (2024). Brasil declara la guerra total a las *fake news. elDiario.es.* Retrieved from <https://www.eldiario.es/internacional/brasil-declara-guerra-total-fake-news_1_11277891.html>.

government's human rights violations.

In Vietnam, after a protest against land grabbing turned violent, the government's cyber-army, called Force 47, flooded social media with forced confessions to silence critics of the government's handling of the situation.

In West Papua, the government uses online manipulation and cyber-attacks to silence civil society and independent media to maintain control over the population's narrative of the struggle for independence from Indonesia[80].

In Myanmar, the algorithm of Facebook was key to promoting the genocide of Rohinya.[81] Etc, etc.

---

80. Innovation for Change. Civicus. (2021). *Hijacking and Weaponizing the Narrative: Disinformation Amid Rising Repression in East Asia*. Retrieved from <https://eastasia. innovationforchange.net/story/hijacking-and-weaponizing-the-narrative-disinformation-amid-rising-repression-in-east-asia/>.

81. Amnesty International. (31 October 2023). *Myanmar: Facebook's systems promoted violence against Rohingya; Meta owes reparations – new report*. Retrieved from < https://www.amnesty.org/en/latest/news/2022/09/myanmar-facebooks-systems-promoted-violence-against-rohingya-meta-owes-reparations-new-report/>.

Part 1. Conclusion: everywhere, anywhere, anytime, all the time

Let us make sure that no one mixes up institutional abuse and business with free speech.

These well-known cases are just paradigmatic examples of common practices around the world. All political parties, their sponsors and clients invest, both online and offline, directly or through others in covert *advertising* (i.e. propaganda), which is as personalised as possible.

Thus, the real cause of fake news and systemic disinformation is to be found within these factors. This means it is *sponsored* information.

It seems paradoxical that the first initiatives to combat recent disinformation have come from social media displays of 'goodwill' rather than from democratic governments, who do little more than feign stupefied indignation and accuse others of their own behaviours. The same tactics of the political parties that form such governments are problematic because they are aimed at manipulating —not persuading— the potential audience of the messages they want to convey. They do not seek to inform or publicise a particular argument or point of view but are aimed at 'artificially' generating echo chambers where the popularity of the party's viewpoint is over-represented, giving users who are part of those bubbles the sensation that theirs is a majority view, generating a pathological social polarisation.

As Mark Scott, chief technology correspondent of Politico in the Brussels' political bubble, said:

> People always ask me: "What are the major concerns of generative AI on misinformation?" Alex Engler, an AI expert at the Brookings Institution, told me. "And I respond that they'll distract us from the fact that platforms have laid off their integrity teams." His point is this: Can artificial intelligence make misinformation worse? Yes. But in the big scheme of things — especially when high-profile politicians with massive online followings can put out falsehoods, mostly unchecked— it's a sideshow that has blinded officials to massive ongoing problems related to social media[82].

---

82. Scott, M. (4 Octuber 2024). Why Western democracy faces a nightmare made

This is a pretty nuanced argument. So please stick with me. No one is saying that AI-generated falsehoods (be they videos, text or images) aren't a problem. It's just that, given the state of social media, they are fringe issues to the main event: a decade-long polarisation that has left the online world segmented along party lines; increasingly fragmented between multiple social networks; and where politicians remain the main purveyors of falsehoods[83]. Into that complex mix, artificial intelligence just isn't going to move the needle beyond making existing problems worse. It's also worth remembering that AI isn't exactly a new thing when it comes to social media. Those pesky recommendation systems from which content pops up into people's feeds have been around for a while —and remain massively problematic in terms of the lack of transparency on how they work. As much as it's easy to get overcome by the generative AI crazy (who doesn't like a deepfake video, amirite?), a greater focus on how those complex recommendation algorithms work would do a lot more to quell potential harmful material than shifting everyone's exclusive attention to a smattering of AI-generated falsehoods.

Don't get me wrong; those things are now entering the wild. Republican presidential candidate Ron DeSantis used an AI-generated voice of Donald Trump in a recent attack ad. Donald Tusk, the opposition leader in the upcoming Polish parliamentary election, used the technology to mimic the voice of the country's prime minister. In other regimes like Venezuela's, the government used off-the-shelf AI technology to put out fake news stories, relying on online avatars, to peddle propaganda. These examples may grab people's attention. But it's not where the real action is ahead.

There is another good reason to claim responsibility from the institutions: if they would lie less, people would need less to look for alternatives even through conspiranoia[84].

online. *POLITICO*. Retrieved from <https://www.politico.eu/article/western-democracy-us-uk-eu-elections-2024-faces-nightmare-social-media-online/>.

83. Reuters Institute For The Study Of Journalism (n.d.). *Politicians across Africa use social media to target their critics. Platforms are complicit.* Retrieved from <https://reutersinstitute.politics.ox.ac.uk/news/politicians-across-africa-use-social-media-target-their-critics-platforms-are-complicit>.

84. Elsevier Ltd. (16 April 2022) The LANCET Vol 399. Retrieved from < https://www.thelancet.com/journals/lancet/article/PIIS0140-6736(22)00172-6/fulltext>. <https://www.thelancet.com/action/showPdf?pii=S0140-6736%2822%2900172-6>.
Salas, J., Salas, J., & Salas, J. (23 February 2022). La confianza, un factor decisivo para resolver el *misterio epidemiolýgico* de la covid. *El País*. Retrieved from <https://elpais.com/ciencia/2022-02-23/la-confianza-un-factor-decisivo-para-resolver-el-misterio-epidemiologico-de-la-covid.html>.

Like information, *conspiranoia*[85] has always existed. It is not enough to demonstrate that it has no foundation. We must accept its challenge. Conspiranoia diagnoses a blind spot in the system[86], i.e. part of something that is truly felt; it speaks of the void it fills. We must understand the needs it satisfies and then work to satisfy them in a different way[87].

At the same time systematic disinformation, propaganda, and conspiranoia have the same role of defending the system because they distract from the real structural problems. They give short-term responses to fears and people's need to believe they are informed, superior and in control of the situation. The impulse that gives rise to conspiranoia is initially healthy ("they are oppressing me / lying to me")[88]. The problem is the process that takes that impulse away from the struggle to change things. The conspiracy theory starts from the lack of answers, in other words, real answers that are not propaganda by the system.

At the same time, the system magnifies the conspiracy theory as the only antagonist and contributes to the deviation from the real problem to silence the subsequent antagonism. It needs it as a distracting antagonist, although in many cases, it will end up devouring it. This is short-termism, again.

As Adam Curtis explains in his work *Can't Get You Out of My Head* (2021)[89], it was someone deeply in the system, James Carothers Garrison, district attorney of Orleans Parish involved in the Kennedy case, who set the bases of the structure with which contemporary conspiranoias are replicated: to uncover a conspiracy, you don't have to look for real clues because they are precisely the ones the conspiracy hides. To uncover it, you have to find patterns of behaviour. Thus,

---

85. In this booklet we will use *Conspiranoia* and not *conspiracy theory* because conspiracies exists, but in here we want to refer only to theories based in paranoia and not reality.

86. *Ibidem.*

87. Wu Ming 1. (2021). Q de Qomplotto. Retrieved from <https://www.wumingfoundation.com/giap/2021/03/q-di-qomplotto/>.

88. *Ibidem.*

89. Curtis, A. (2021). *Can't Get You Out of My Head.* Retrieved from <https://archive.org/details/adamcurtis2021>.

almost anything can be suspicious.

In the face of the real problem of systemic propaganda from different ideological factions defining reality according to their convenience, the most backward, conservative and animal diffidence comes to replace intelligence.

One of the most ancestral human desires is to belong to a group. This has permitted most of the great atrocities in history. Identifying an outside enemy reinforces the group. There is a conservative physiological component in preferring to avoid the effort of understanding to return to safe and tangible places. Truth is difficult to reach and is not worth the effort in a postmodern mental framework where the *neutrality* of everyone being able to have their own truth is accepted, as if subjectivity and objectivity were the same. This is what allows the law of the strongest to prevail in the end.

PART 2

Current Approaches To Disinformation
And Why They Do Not Work

1. Biases in the definition of fake news and disinfomation

Segregation of the Internet: politics is busy with *online disinformation*. Why is that? Do they prefer the usual offline disinformation?

There is an open discussion on terminology. Some hold that fake news is not a helpful term to define disinformation, mainly for two reasons: firstly, they consider it an inadequate or insufficient concept, as it does not capture the full complexity of the forms of information manipulation, which includes information that is not strictly speaking false or fake. Secondly, because the term can currently lead to confusion, as powerful actors have appropriated it to delegitimise truthful but inconvenient information and attack rigorous sources, purely because they are critical. For this reason, some reject the term *fake news*, preferring *disinformation*.

In this booklet, we use both terms. We do not want to renounce *fake news*, which has consolidated itself to meme-like status and permeated today's pop culture, allowing us, with just two words, to connect with audiences and make perfectly clear what we are referring to. *Disinformation*, on the other hand, is a more rigorous and therefore equally useful term.

How have the concepts of truth and lies been refined and developed throughout history? What follows is a brief overview of what this propaganda discipline has served. In other words, the imposition of 'truth'.

The definition of *disinformation* as a diversionary manoeuvre

The Oxford English Dictionary defines the term *misinformation* as *Wrong or misleading information* and traces the first English-language reference as The Times, 3 June 1955. It suggests that the term *perhaps* derives from Russian, *дезинформация* (transliterated as *dezinformacija*), first recorded in 1949 (whereas the French equivalent *désinformation* was not recorded until 1954)[90]. More recently, the various aspects, origins and reasons behind disinformation have been explored in greater depth, proposing segmented distinctions.

Many current definitions identify disinformation where there is an intention to cause harm or to achieve political or financial gain.

We understand the intention of this separation: that ordinary people who express themselves without the capacity to professionally elaborate information should not be targets in the pursuit of disinformation. However, we suggest pursuing the same strategies by switching the focus, clearly distinguishing between those who express themselves without paying or receiving payment for it, and those who don't, or are institutions. With this separation in mind, we are inclined to treat cases of unintentional systematic and systemic malpractice similarly to cases of intentionally false news, as they both result in unverified information being presented, and they may have a similar or greater impact.

This is also because we do not wish to lend weight to the arguments of institutions that, to save their own skins, insist we must distinguish between *information failure* or *misinformation* and *disinformation*. They claim that sometimes they make *mistakes*. However, in the case of institutions and other similar big fish in the information business, we will not accept non-verification as a *mistake*. It is a failure in their duty.

There is a clear bias in favour of the status quo's specific monopolistic interests, which prioritise their objectives over a genuine search for solutions and —more seriously —over the fundamental rights and freedoms of expression and access to information for everyone, not just them.

This is the case, for example, in the work on disinformation started in April 2018 by the European Commission, with the Report of the High-Level Expert Group on Fake News and Online Disinformation, gathering the 'opinion' of representatives and experts from the 28 EU countries[91].

---

90. Bentzen, N. (2015). *Understanding propaganda and disinformation.* European Parliamentary Research Service. Retrieved from <https://www.europarl.europa.eu/RegData/etudes/ATAG/2015/571332/EPRS_ATA(2015)571332_EN.pdf>

91. High level Group on fake news and online disinformation.2018. (April 2018). *A multi-dimensional approach to disinformation.* Directorate-General for Communications

In 2022 the US tried something similar that failed[92].

The EU report from the High-Level Expert Group on Fake News and Online Disinformation is not some trivial document but forms the basis for EU policy on the issue, and is updated frequently. Despite the appearance of infallibility given by its somewhat pompous name, this is a highly problematic document. The title itself, which refers specifically to technology (*online*), ignores the fact that disinformation is not limited to the Internet; technophobia does not solve the issue at hand; in fact, quite the opposite.

Since the first version, the report clearly and intentionally reproduces a bias that excludes the historical – offline— producers of fake news from the problem: the aforementioned governments, institutions, political parties, corporations, fortunes, and media. Anecdotally, the monopolistic and paternalistic matrix of the report becomes even more evident when we take into account the positive assessment it offers of the then-incipient "Directive on copyright and related rights in the Digital Single Market", which included aspects criticised as curtailing freedoms[93,94,95] as if copyright bore any relation to guarantees of truthfulness. If there is any relationship between these two areas in Europe, it is not the relationship that the report seems to imply. Instead, it is one in which the journalism industry does not pay royalties to journalists, thanks to such misleading copyright-fanatics laws, rendering the profession ever more precarious. This forces journalists to work in conditions where they lack sufficient time to comply with the most basic standards of ethics and verification.

Networks, Content and Technology (European Commission). ISBN 978-92-79-80420-5. DOI 10.2759/739290. Retrieved from <https://op.europa.eu/en/publication-detail/-/publi-cation/6ef4df8b-4cea-11e8-be1d-01aa75ed71a1>.

92. *Disinformation Governance Board* (28 April 2022). in *Wikipedia.* Retrieved from <https://en.wikipedia.org/wiki/Disinformation_Governance_Board>.

93. Xnet. 2019. (March 2019.) *On the passing of the Copyright Directive: Don't call it censorship, call it copyright.* Retrieved from <https://xnet-x.net/es/aprobacion-directi-va-copyright-no-llames-censura-llamalo-derechos-autor/>.

94. Communia, the International Association On the Digital Public Domain. (n.d.) *Internet is for the people.* Retrieved from <https://reform.communia-association.org/>.

95. European Union. (2019). Directive (EU) 2019/790 of the European Parliament and of the Council of 17 April 2019 on copyright and related rights in the Digital Single Market and amending Directives 96/9/EC and 2001/29/EC. Retrieved from <https://eur-lex.europa.eu/eli/dir/2019/790/oj>

There is also an insistence on excluding *unintentionally erroneou* information, ostensibly to protect *the people*; in reality, this serves to exclude the malpractice of the bulk of its members. Although at first glance, this may appear to be an approach founded on civil rights, in reality, it is mainly a consequence of the massive presence of media lobbies in decision-making surrounding the issue of fake news.

One only has to look at the unbalanced composition of the group of experts chosen by the European Commission for this Group, formed of 39 *experts* (see Figure 1) from more than 300 nominations that excludes, without explanation, proposed candidates such as the UN rapporteur on freedom of expression, David Kaye. In addition, the Committee is chaired by Madeleine de Cock Buning, a specialist in... intellectual property in the media.

Some 46% of its members are directly or indirectly linked to the large information conglomerates[96].

It would not be far-fetched to think that the goal of most members of this Group might be, rather than a selfless concern for improving democracy, more a matter of preserving their privileges in the face of democratisation of access to and creation of information as a result of digital culture.

In the same vein of saving their skin and, preserving the status quo of producers of mass disinformation, pointing the finger of blame at "individual citizens or groups of citizens", the report makes such statements as:

> Problems of disinformation are deeply intertwined with the development of digital media. They are driven by actors - state or non-state political actors, for-profit actors, media, citizens, individually or in groups —and by manipulative uses of communication infrastructures[99].

As we can see, considerable effort has been poured into stoking up fear of digital.

---

96. High level Group on fake news and online disinformation. 2018. (April 2018.) op. cit.

97. Page 6, High level Group on fake news and online disinformation. (April 2018). op. cit.

NOMBRE	CARGO/ORGANISMO/COMPAÑÍA
Raag, Ilmar	**Ejecutivo de medios**
Bechmann, Anja	Universidad de Aarhus
Nielsen, Rasmus	Instituto Reuters para el Estudio del Periodismo (Universidad de Oxford)
Markovski, Veni	Experto en internet
Jiménez Cruz, Clara	**Maldita.es/El Objetivo, de La Sexta**
Frau-Meigs, Divina	Universidad Sorbona Nueva
Pollicino, Oreste	Universidad Bocconi
Vaisbrode, Neringa	**Asesor de comunicación**
Rozukalne, Anda	Universidad Rīga Stradiņš
Bargaoanu, Alina	Universidad de Bucarest
Turk, Ziga	Universidad de Liubliana
Curran, Noel	**Unión Europea de Radiodifusión**
Gniffke, Kai	**ARD**
Schwetje, Sonja	**Grupo RTL**
Nieri, Gina	**Mediaset**
Stjarne, Hanna	**Sveriges Television**
Polák, Juraj	**RTVS**
Whitehead, Sarah	**Sky News**
Goyens, Monique	Organización Europea del Consumidor
Steenfadt, Olaf	Reporteros sin fronteras
Sundermann, Marc	**Bertelsmann & Co**
Von Reppert-Bismarck, Juliane	Lie Detectors
Mantzarlis, Alexios	International Fact-Checking Network (Instituto Poynter)
Salo, Mikko	Faktabaari
Dzsinich, Gergely	Cybersecurity and cybercrime Advisors Network
Riotta, Gianni	**Periodista**
Niklewicz, Konrad	Civic Institute
Wardle, Claire	First draft
Dimitrov, Dimitar	Wikimedia
MacDonald, Raegan	Mozilla Firefox
Lundblad, Nicklas	*Google*
Turner, Stephen	*Twitter*
Allan, Richard	*Facebook*
Gutiérrez, Ricardo	Federación Europea de Periodistas
Leclercq, Christophe	EurActiv
Lemarchand, Grégoire	**Agence France-Presse**
Rae, Stephen	**Independent News and Media**
Fubini, Federico	Periodista
Wijk, Wout van	**News Media Europe**

The composition[98] of the first High-Level Expert Committee set up by the European Commission. Names linked directly or indirectly to large information conglomerates (in bold) or content dissemination conglomerates (in italics) have been marked. They represent 46% of the committee members. Members with advanced knowledge of the functioning of what is defined in the title as 'online' represent only 21%.

In conclusion, a light should be shone on the fact that any attempt

---

98. *Ibid.*, pag 39.

to define and describe the situation is problematic if the key players, complicit in the problem-creation, are excluded from the analysis. The systemic narrative on disinformation omits the traditional tactics used to their advantage by the established political, economic, and information ecosystems to gain both wealth and public favour that can be translated into votes and decision-making power.

The major disinformation generators take advantage of the digital environment and the democratisation it permits, just as they have done with all the other spaces they monopolise. When we accept the segregation of the disinformation problem in the online sphere by entrenching technophobic platitudes, we contribute to a narrative that favours a state of exception on the Internet and hinders the exercise of civil rights online.

Modalities of falsehoods and human nature

As described above, disinformation occurs not only when a news item is entirely false and fabricated. In fact, in most cases, there are other forms of misrepresentation, such as

> • cherry picking (the selective collection of data to support the thesis being defended)
> • inflated statistics and data
> • data or information offered out of context
> • Treating information from unreliable sources as accurate
> • the use of isolated cases as if they were the general rule
> • "broken telephone" style stories, which are passed on with slight modifications made at each stage
> • political or moral assertions that are taken as given without question
> • the presentation of facts as the result of a definite relationship when they are only related in time and space by chance or coincidence, etc.

None of these forms of disinformation are unique to or original to the Internet; instead, they are inherent to human nature. As humans, we tend to select information that reaffirms our beliefs and pass on information to convince others. As said, such psychological biases have been, and remain to date, enthusiastically amplified by systemic propaganda throughout every age of humanity, so that fake news has spread faster than real news in most cases[99].

Authoritative researchers have confirmed the idea that disinformation is not predominantly an online phenomenon. In *Emotions, Partisanship, and Misperceptions: How Anger and Anxiety Moderate the Effect of Partisan Bias on Susceptibility to Political Misinformation*[100], Brian E. Weeks analyses how erroneous beliefs about the political sphere are related to citizens' emotional experiences, how they are linked to anxiety and anger, and how parties operate in this psychological field.
In *Denying to the Grave: Why We Ignore the Facts That Will Save Us*[101], Sara and Jack Gorman demonstrate the scientific hypothesis that human nature leads to denial in some matters. In this respect, the Internet is just another tool to enhance confirmation bias; it is neither the only such tool nor the first, as it is inherent to human beings. Processing information that supports beliefs we already hold gives us pleasure.

Because of the prevailing technophobic narrative, many people instinctively think of disinformation as an online problem, but all its categories can also be found offline:

It is striking that there is little difference in self-reported exposure to misinformation between those who mainly consume news offline and those who mainly consume news online…. More striking still is that, in the US, self-reported exposure to entirely made-up news stories is more widespread among those who mainly consume news offline (36%, compared to 29% for those who mainly consume news online). When we dig deeper into the data, we see that this is mainly due to

right-wingers consuming a lot of 24-hour TV news[102].

99. Vosoughi, S., Roy, D., and Aral, S. 2018. *The spread of true and false news online*, Science, 359(6380), pp.1146-1151, DOI: 10.1126/science.aap9559. Retrieved from <https://www.science.org/doi/10.1126/science.aap9559>.

100. Weeks, B. E. 2015. Emotions, Partisanship, and Misperceptions: How Anger and Anxiety Moderate the Effect of Partisan Bias on Susceptibility to Political Misinformation, *Journal of Communication*, ISSN 0021-9916, 65(4), pp. 699-719. Retrieved from <https://doi.org/10.1111/jcom.12164>.

101. Gorman, S. E., and Gorman, J. M. 2017. *Denying to the Grave: Why We Ignore the Facts that Will Save Us*. New York. Oxford University Press. ISBN-13: 978-0199396603, ISBN-10: 0199396604.

102. Newman, N., Fletcher, R., Kalogeropoulos, A., Levy D.A.L., and Nielsen, R.K.

According to Freedom House's *Freedom on the Net 2017* report[103], based on an analysis of seventeen electoral processes in various countries, governments and political and economic elites are the leading producers of political disinformation online:

> Governments worldwide have dramatically increased their efforts to manipulate information on social media over the past year. The Chinese and Russian regimes pioneered the use of covert methods to distort online discussions and suppress dissent more than a decade ago, but the practice has since gone global....
>
> Manipulation and disinformation tactics played an important role in elections in at least 17 other countries over the past year.... Although some governments sought to support their interests and expand their influence abroad —as with Russia's disinformation campaigns in the United States and Europe— in most cases, they used these methods inside their borders to maintain their hold on power[104].

The findings of professors Hunt Allcott, New York University, and Matthew Gentzkow, Stanford University, and members of the National Bureau of Economic Research (NBER) - based on 1200 online respondents - show that social networks "are a major but not dominant source" of information. Only 14% of respondents considered social media their most important source of information in elections. The study also found that a fake news story would have to have the same effect as 36 television advertisements to change the way people vote. Let us not forget that conspiracy theories have always existed[105].

In *Troops, Trolls and Troublemakers: A Global Inventory of Organised*

(2018). *Digital News Report 2018*. Reuters Institute for the Study of Journalism. ISBN 978-1-907384-46-2. Retrieved from <https://reutersinstitute.politics.ox.ac.uk/sites/default/files/digital-news-report-2018.pdf>.

103. Kelly, S., Truong, M., Shahbaz, A., Earp, M., and White, J. (November 2017). *Freedom on the Net 2017: Manipulating Social Media to Undermine Democracy*. Freedom House Project. Retrieved from <https://freedomhouse.org/sites/default/files/2020-02/FOTN_2017_Final_compressed.pdf>.

104. Kelly, S., Truong, M., Shahbaz, A., Earp, M., and White, J. (November 2017). Page 1. op. cit.

105. Allcott, H., and Gentzkow, M. (2017), op. cit.

Social Media Manipulation[106], Samantha Bradshaw and Philip N. Howard of Oxford University find that it is states in authoritarian countries and parties and similar organisations in democracies that organise armies of trolls for domestic audiences. What was a developing phenomenon in 2010 can now be found in at least 28 countries. Furthermore, to debunk another myth, cases in which manipulation through trolls has been used to attack other governments are in the minority; they are most commonly used for domestic consumption.

An action-oriented definition of *Disinformation*

In conclusion, it is impossible to tackle this issue seriously if certain actors are not included in the analysis. Firstly, the definition of disinformation must include all the systemic ways information is manipulated to serve one interest or another, either voluntarily or due to the inertia of malpractice. Secondly, we must be aware that behind the disinformation that gives structure to that-which-is-commonly-accepted is a status quo of mass generators of disinformation, not primarily ordinary people and their right to freedom of expression. We are nothing more than instruments or useful scapegoats.

For all these reasons, the definition of 'disinformation' proposed in this book is as follows:

Disinformation includes fake news and inaccurate, manipulated or misleading information. When we use freedom of expression, we can consider this an imperfect and inherent part of our human nature, which in itself does not have enough reach to be the source of mass public harm. However, such public harm is caused when financial or institutional resources are involved in creating and viralising disinformation, be it online or offline and in traditional formats. In such cases, it must be seriously sanctioned and eradicated to safeguard democratic rights and freedoms.

---

106. Bradshaw, S., and Howard, P. N. (2017). *Troops, Trolls and Troublemakers: A Global Inventory of Organized Social Media Manipulation.* Computational Propaganda Research Project, Oxford Internet Institute, Working Paper no. 2017.12. Retrieved from <https://demtech.oii.ox.ac.uk/wp-content/uploads/sites/89/2017/07/Troops-Trolls-and-Troublemakers.pdf>.

2. Legislative moods that damage civil rights and freedoms

At this point, we have established that there is a disinformation industry and that among the major producers who grease its cogs are the actors who should stop it by creating a regulatory framework. They are unlikely to put much effort into doing so unless the public forcefully demands it, since doing so would harm them directly by reducing their power of influence.

So, not surprisingly, the practical and legal path that we propose later in this booklet goes in the opposite direction to the one pursued by governments up till now. However, it is aligned with an institutional document that, by the way, these same governments systematically ignore: the Joint Declaration on Freedom of Expression and *Fake News*, Disinformation and Propaganda by the United Nations Special Rapporteur on Freedom of opinion and expression, David Kaye, along with his counterparts from the Organization for Security and Co-operation in Europe (OSCE), the Organization of American States (OAS), and the African Commission on Human and Peoples' Rights (ACHPR)[107].

This declaration underlines the critical role of the Internet in responding to disinformation. Moreover, it warns of public policies denigrating the media, blurring the lines between disinformation and independent information based on verifiable facts. The signatories to the Declaration regret attempts by states to suppress dissent and control public communications by, for example, *privatising* oversight measures by placing pressure on intermediaries to act by restricting content, measures that are generally opaque and which constrain the legitimate exercise of freedom of expression and information. The Declaration establishes some general guidelines that must be respected to fight

---

107. United Nations (UN) Special Rapporteur on Freedom of Opinion and Expression, Organization for Security and Co-operation in Europe (OSCE) Representative on Freedom of the Media, Organization of American States (OAS) Special Rapporteur on Freedom of Expression, and African Commission on Human and Peoples' Rights (ACHPR) Special Rapporteur on Freedom of Expression and Access to Information. (3 March 2017). *Joint Declaration on Freedom of Expression and Fake News, Disinformation and Propaganda*. Retrieved from <https://www.osce.org/files/f/documents/6/8/302796.pdf>..

disinformation and warns against basing legislation on ambiguous concepts such as *truth* or *lies*, or introducing liberticidal control-based policies.

Between 2011 and 2023, 78 countries[108] passed laws on disinformation. Some advances have been made in transparency, but most bills erode fundamental rights.

In the US, the Countering Foreign Propaganda and Disinformation Act (2016) is mainly designed to combat foreign propaganda, but also introduces ways to weaken the interpretation of domestic propaganda protections. These laws prevent the US Department of State from gathering information to develop targeted propaganda and explicitly attempting to influence opinions. In the National Defence Authorization Act for Fiscal Year, since 2017[109], in Section 1287 and others of this pervasive law, we find the creation of the Global Engagement Center within the Secretary of State's Office. This centre aims to synchronise and coordinate the Federal Government's efforts to "recognise, understand, expose, and counter foreign state and non-state propaganda and disinformation efforts aimed at undermining United States national security interests".

Beyond these strategic political and security-focused measures, the US Congress considered a bill on advertising: the Honest Ads Act[110]. This initiative sought to improve the transparency and accountability of those who buy and publish political advertisements online by requiring them to disclose detailed information. The Supreme Court has recognised the right of the electorate to be fully informed[111]. Since 2002, the United States has had a regulation that establishes transparency requirements

---

108. Monir, M. (21 July 2023). *Chilling Legislation: Tracking the Impact of "Fake News" Laws on Press Freedom Internationally - Center for International Media Assistance.* Center For International Media Assistance. Retrieved from <https://www.cima.ned.org/publication/chilling-legislation/>.

109. National Defense Authorization Act for Fiscal Year 2017, H.R.2810. Retrieved from <https://www.congress.gov/114/plaws/publ328/PLAW-114publ328.pdf>.

110. Honest Ads Act, S.1356 —116th Congress (2019-2020). Retrieved from <https://www.congress.gov/bill/116th-congress/senate-bill/1356/text>.

111. Citizens United v. Federal Election Commission, No. 08-205 U.S. Supreme Court (2009). Retrieved from <https://www.supremecourt.gov/opinions/09pdf/08-205.pdf>. <https://www.law.cornell.edu/supct/html/08-205.ZO.html>.

for political advertisements broadcast on television or radio[112]. The Honest Ads Act was intended to include actors not covered by the 2002 law. Two findings are essential to justify the proposal: on the one hand, free and fair elections require transparency and accountability to ensure the public's right to know the authentic sources of political ad financing and to make informed political decisions; on the other hand, transparency of political ad financing is essential to ensure compliance with other campaign finance laws, such as the prohibition of foreign nationals from financing campaigns.

Finally, it is also interesting that on 1 July 2019, California became the first US state to regulate bots. It requires them to disclose their 'artificial identity' when they are programmed to sell a product or influence a voter[113]. Just as pharmaceutical companies must disclose that happy people who claim a new drug has miraculously improved their lives are, in fact, hired actors. In California, bots, or rather people who hire them for political or commercial campaigns, must clearly identify themselves and ensure their programming is reasonable.
Continuing in this direction, with the Algorithmic Justice and Online Platform Transparency Act 2021[114], steps are being taken at the national level to improve transparency on how and why certain information is displayed to users of online platforms and on content moderation.

A case study: how European institutions deal with disinformation

Beautified by the famous High-Level Expert Group, which has already been criticised at length in the first part of this booklet, the predominant EU focus is based on *external enemies*, self-regulation and co-regulation. It attributes great responsibility and thus the power to intermediaries, in this case mainly online platforms, opening the door to privatised control of freedom of expression, i.e. an updated but classical form of systemic censorship. The economic strategies are directed towards education

---

112. *Stand by Your Ad provision*. (n.d.). in Wikipedia. Retrieved from <https://en.wikipedia.org/wiki/Stand_by_Your_Ad_provision>.

113. State of California. Bots: disclosure. SB 1001. (2018). Retrieved from <https://leginfo.legislature.ca.gov/faces/billTextClient.xhtml?bill_id=201720180SB1001>.

114. Algorithmic Justice and Online Platform Transparency Act, S.1896 — 117th Congress (2021-2022). Retrieved from <https://www.congress.gov/bill/117th-congress/senate-bill/1896/text>.

on media literacy and fact-checking initiatives, which are good but not structurally enough[115]. Nevertheless, it also points out certain unavoidable principles that we can use to support the thesis proposed in this booklet and which are helpful to leverage a policy change.

From the outset - and with mitigations only from 2021 onwards, when for the first time the word *offline* is also associated with disinformation[116] —the tendency is to stigmatise new technologies that can be used to "disseminate disinformation on a scale and with speed and precision of targeting that is unprecedented"[117]. This, while accurate, is equally true for television and for the circulation of other types of information, such as the truths they do not want to hear. According to their interpretation, this is detrimental to media pluralism. In other words, these arguments are used to say that the media never lies and that it is the media, not individuals, who are the natural custodians of freedom of expression, as well as to claim that the only culprit is the digital danger, instead of identifying it as something caused by the self-interest of institutions, parties and other players on the political stage.

However, to reinforce our own proposal, it is worth detailing some of the concrete measures that the Commission and its Expert Group propose, which are actually useful and mostly self-regulatory without enforcement obligations.

Firstly —although limited to Internet platforms at least until 2021[118]— it recommends transparency in the provision of political information through the following mechanisms:

115. Alex Tabarrok (2022). *Fact Checking Increases Fake News*. Retrieved from <https://marginalrevolution.com/marginalrevolution/2022/06/fact-checking-increases-fake-news.html>.

116. European Commission. (25 November 2021). *European Democracy: Commission sets out new laws on political advertising, electoral rights and party funding* [PRESS RELEASE]. Brussels. Retrieved from <https://ec.europa.eu/commission/presscorner/detail/en/ip_21_6118>.

117. European Commission. (26 April 2018). *Communication from the Commission to the European Parliament, the Council, the European Economic and Social Committee and the Committee of the Regions. Tackling online disinformation: a European Approach*. COM(2018) 236 final. Retrieved from <https://eur-lex.europa.eu/legal-content/EN/TXT/?uri=CELEX:52018DC0236>.

118. European Commission. (25 November 2021), op. cit.

> clearly labelling content that has been paid for and is being promoted as part of a campaign, and making contextual information, including the originators and online amplifiers of false news, available to users and for research and transparency purposes[119].

Note that since then, Google, Facebook and Twitter have already applied these measures. The measures seem appropriate, but it makes no sense that they have been defended in the mainstream political narrative as applying especially during electoral campaigns. There is no reason why the toxic and partisan information we receive all year round, outside of election campaigns, should not be of equal concern. In 2021, it is beginning to be considered that targeting criteria should be made public, although we still need to get them banned. Only timid attempts are being made to provide exceptions in the case of minors in the EU. At the same time, the United States has had a regulation that establishes transparency requirements for political advertisements broadcast on television or radio since 2002[120] with the aforementioned Honest Ads Act (2020)[121].

Secondly, some actions are envisaged to increase the transparency of funding sources, in particular. *All digital media* (again only digital) should:

> provide the necessary information to help the reader to identify who is behind a certain type of information. [...]. Sponsored content has to be clearly identifiable [...]" especially political content. "Furthermore, it is important that advertising is not inadvertently funding disinformation [...] Information on payments to human influencers and use of robots to promote a certain message should be made available in order for users to understand whether the apparent popularity of a given piece of online information or the apparent popularity of an influencer is the result of artificial amplification or is supported by targeted investments[122].

---

119. High Level Group on fake news and online disinformation. (2018). *A multidimensional approach to disinformation*. Publications Office of the European Union. March 2018, page 22. Retrieved from <https://op.europa.eu/en/publication-detail/-/publication/6ef4df8b-4cea-11e8-be1d-01aa75ed71a1#>.

120. *Stand by Your Ad provision*. (n.d.). in Wikipedia. Retrieved from <https://en.wikipedia.org/wiki/Stand_by_Your_Ad_provision>.

121. Honest Ads Act, S.1356 — 116th Congress, 2019-2020. Retrieved from <https://www.congress.gov/bill/116th-congress/senate-bill/1356/text>.

122. Honest Ads Act, S.1356 — 116th Congress, 2019-2020. Retrieved from <https://www.congress.gov/bill/116th-congress/senate-bill/1356/text>.

The Commission suggests increasing transparency about the origin of information and how it is produced, sponsored, and disseminated to allow citizens to assess the online content they access and expose possible attempts to manipulate opinion.

Recently the EU has approved the European Media Freedom Act (EMFA)[123] that will come into force in August 2025. The Regulation (Article 6) obliges media outlets to publish information about their owners, and about the income they receive from advertising from publicentities. Furthermore, Article 25 obliges public bodies to publish detailed data on the distribution of institutional advertising, a distribution that must be done according to "transparent, objective criteria, proportionate and non-discriminatory."

Specifically, the principles that make up the European Commission's code of good practice[124] include that of "reducing revenues of the purveyors of disinformation".

We need to be careful, however, when this implies that someone is qualified to say who is lying and who is not, and that it is taken for granted that the one who decides is not a liar. It is taken for granted that some will get rich and others will see "their revenues reduced". In practice, this has already materialised: in many countries, online platforms get rich and, at the same time, remove content without wasting much time in avoiding "the censoring of critical, satirical, dissenting, or shocking speech"[125] or respecting an *open Internet*[126]. On the contrary, they do not allow the publication of links to independent blogs and only consider 'truthful news', in other words that which originates from the mainstream media, the pre-digital monopolies of disinformation. Thus, they contribute to achieving the objective of preserving the status quo and the existing interests of the information corporations, as suggested by the composition of the initial High-Level Expert Group discussed in previous chapters.

---

123. European Union. (11 April 2024). *Regulation (eu) 2024/1083 of the european parliament and of the council.* Official Journal of the European Union. Retrieved from <https://eur-lex.europa.eu/legal-content/EN/TXT/?uri=OJ%3AL_202401083>.

124. European Commission. (2018). *EU Code of Practice on Disinformation.* Retrieved from <https://digital-strategy.ec.europa.eu/en/policies/code-practice-disinformation>.

125. European Commission. (26 April 2018), op. cit.

126. *Ibidem.*

This *media exemption* comes back over and over again in different forms, like the discussion on Digital Service Act[127] or in the text of EMFA (Article 17)[128] in the European Institutions where the *real media*, following their own definition, are exempt from major moderation rules.

Another principle is to

> ensure transparency about sponsored content, particularly political and issue-based advertising; this should be complemented by repositories where comprehensive information about sponsored content is provided, such as the actual sponsor identity, amounts spent and targeting criteria used. Similar mechanisms should be implemented so that users understand why they have been targeted by a given advertisement[129].

In addition, the Commission notes that

> some platforms have taken on functions traditionally associated with media outlets, entering the news business as content aggregators and distributors without necessarily taking on the editorial frameworks and capabilities of such outlets[130].

(i.e. new entrants that do not fact-check are in the way of a long-established monopoly that does not necessarily fact-check either).

Furthermore, it considers that users play an active role in the spread of disinformation, especially in terms of sharing content without verifying it first. According to the Commission —in a paternalistic approach towards citizens, with a rationale that leads to private censorship on digital platforms— online platforms should take the lead in countering disinformation, so that they are responsible for protecting users against fake news. What is hard to understand is why, if we take the premise that online platforms are trying to occupy mainstream media spaces, only online platforms should be held responsible and not the media that

---

127. Xnet. (2023). *Paquete de Servicios Digitales (DSA), el an6lisis de Xnet.* Xnet — Internet, Derechos y Democracia En la Era Digital. https://xnet-x.net/es/posicion-xnet-dsa-package/

128. EU DisinfoLab. (n. d.) *The European Commission's EMFA proposal is paving the way for the media exemption to come back.* EU DisinfoLab. Retrieved from <https://www.disinfo.eu/advocacy/the-european-commissions-emfa-proposal-is-paving-the-way-for-the-media-exemption-to-come-back/>.

129. *Ibid.*, pag 49.

130. *Ibid.*, pag 49.

previously occupied these spaces.

Bearing all the above in mind, it seems that the Commission's focus is on the distributors and recipients of disinformation rather than on its promoters and sponsors.

As far as commercial communications are concerned, EU law obliges Member States to ensure that these communications comply with several conditions, including that the natural or legal person on behalf of whom commercial communications are made must be clearly identifiable. In this context, it is striking to note the effort and propaganda poured into creating a new specific legislative framework when, in this particular case, it is redundant with respect to the existing European legislation.

The European Audiovisual Media Directive[131] also includes elements that, if enforced, would be helpful:

> Transparency of media ownership is directly linked to freedom of expression, a cornerstone of democratic systems124. [...] To strengthen freedom of expression and, by extension, to promote media pluralism and avoid conflicts of interest, it is important for Member States to ensure that users have easy and direct access at all times to information about media service providers [...][132].

Surprising, is it not? New laws are proposed for new players when current laws are not adequately enforced for long-standing players. Even in the light of the rules outlined above, it is not consistent for the handling of disinformation to adopt selective measures affecting only online platforms. It should also be recalled that freedom of expression applies to commercial and political advertising and sponsorship.
The more digital-conscious legislative wave emerging after the COVID-19 pandemic, such as the Digital Services Act, the Digital Markets Act, the European Democracy Action Plan, etc., has updated all these trends but remains substantially unchanged.

---

131. European Union. (2018). Directive (EU) 2018/1808 of the European Parliament and of the Council of 14 November 2018 amending Directive 2010/13/EU on the coordination of certain provisions laid down by law, regulation or administrative action in Member States concerning the provision of audiovisual media services (Audiovisual Media Services Directive) in view of changing market realities. Retrieved from <https://eur-lex.europa.eu/eli/dir/2018/1808/oj>.

132. Recital 16. European Union. 2018, op. cit.

In 2023, the Digital Service Act (DSA) and Digital Market Act (DMA), a legislative package[133], has passed into law in the EU. Presented as the EU's flagship initiative to demonstrate concrete actions, it brings some improvements but, in many areas, falls short, due to clear pressure from lobbyists[134].

It affects intermediaries who provide information society services, such as: social media platforms; data storage services like cloud and web hosting; network infrastructure providers (internet service providers, domain name registrars); online marketplaces; app stores; and collaborative economy platforms.

Of course, there is nothing on offline disinformation since the legislation is about digital...

The legislation emphasises the obligation for those defined as 'very large online platforms and search engines', meaning those reaching more than 10% of the population. They have more outstanding obligations regarding transparency, risk prevention, and social impacts classified as illicit concerning their recommendation system design or any other algorithmic system, content moderation systems, general terms of service, ad selection systems, and other data-related practices.

Here's a brief overview of what we've gained with this legislation and where it falls short:

It equates political propaganda to advertising (Article 3 r), as we advocate in this book, but the definition of advertising differs from our own. By defining *advertising* as *information designed to promote a message* and disseminated online in exchange for remuneration, it opens the door to widely used propaganda in the form of news.

On the other hand (Article 26), service providers must allow service recipients to clearly, concisely, and unambiguously identify in real-time for each ad that it is an ad, who paid for it, and if it's the same person

---

133. *The Digital Services Act package.* 12 July 2024). Shaping Europe's Digital Future. Retrieved from <https://digital-strategy.ec.europa.eu/en/policies/digital-services-act-package>.

134. Xnet. (2023). *Digital Services Package (DSA), Xnet analysis.* Xnet — Internet, Rights and Democracy in the Digital Age. https://xnet-x.net/es/posicion-xnet-dsa-package/

advertising, the parameters by which they are viewing it and how to change it. As mentioned, this was already done during electoral periods and voluntarily by major platforms, so it's now being applied more broadly.

Intermediary providers are not liable if they do not "select the recipient" (Article 4 b). This is interesting for several reasons. It is important that intermediaries are not responsible for the content of those using their services, because this would turn intermediaries into private censors with broad and massive criteria applied to freedom of expression. However, if an intermediary favours one message over another for users, they are responsible for this choice. It is known that polarising content promotes user engagement. This article is one of the disincentives of the law.

Article 8 explicitly states that users will not be monitored —a positive point against mass surveillance.

In this regard, profiling (GDPR Article 4.4) of users is prohibited (Article 26.3), but it is not permitted only in the case of minors (Article 28). For others, it is only forbidden when special category data such as ethnic or racial origin, political opinions, religious or philosophical beliefs, trade union membership, health data, genetic or biometric data, or sexual orientation is used. I believe that this unwarranted discrimination is justified only if accompanied by a free opt-in option.

Regarding recommendation systems (Article 38), Very Large Online Platforms (VLOPs) and search engine providers using recommendation systems must offer at least one option for each recommendation system that does not rely on profiling. This already exists. Once again, it would be much more respectful of fundamental rights if this were provided without default recommendations and required opt-in.

It aims to tackle user manipulation. Article 25 expressly prohibits dark patterns, i.e. manipulative design of user interfaces, such as giving more prominence to specific options, repeatedly requesting that the service recipient choose an option when that choice has already been made, or making the process to end a service more complex than subscribing to it. Furthermore, Article 14.5 states that large online platform providers and search engines can no longer have incomprehensible terms and conditions spanning dozens of pages. In any case, private platforms still retain significant discretion in determining content illegality.

Lastly, access to information is even more limited than allowed by transparency laws. To obtain information from very large platforms, you not only need to request it but also require authorisation as a researcher (Article 40), when the burden should at least be reversed.

As for the DMA, it has been in effect since May-June 2023 (with fines of up to 20% of turnover), affecting intermediary services, online search engines, social networks, video-sharing platforms, interpersonal communication services, operating systems, browsers, virtual assistants, cloud computing, online advertising services and computer application stores. It introduces the concept of *gatekeepers*. It aims to reduce their influence, i.e. monopolistic concentration, while also preventing data transfer to third parties and significantly expanding interoperability and portability obligations, allowing for broader device configuration without user discrimination and enabling choice in installed and uninstalled programs, thereby improving the position of open-source software.

Nevertheless, in summary, it remains an approach in which platforms are not treated as major recipients of payments, so the kind of responsibility given to them is one of oversight; a kind of privatised authority. The emphasis is therefore not on verification, but on censorship.

Regarding AI, all information done via AI will have to be labelled as such[135]. Good news.

Excepting some light getting through, like in the Irish new bill (2024)[136], which forces all recommender systems based on intimately profiling people to be turned off by default, other recent pieces of legislation are still very weak. For example, the recent Agreement of Online Advertisements (2024), which is full of complexity but does not really go for it, or the mentioned EMFA.

Beyond the European Union, the issue of disinformation has also been extensively addressed by other European actors, notably the Council of

---

135. Franceinfo [@franceinfo] (3 April 2023) *DIRECT - Thierry Breton, commissaire européen au marché intérieur, est l'invité du #8h30franceinfo.* Retrieved from <https://twitter.com/franceinfo/status/1642784539679260672>.

136. Teachout, Z. et al. (2023) The EU should support Ireland's bold move to regulate Big Tech. *The Hill.* Retrieved from <https://blog.quintarelli.it/2023/12/the-eu-should-support-irelands-bold-move-to-regulate-big-tech/>.

Europe, the international organisation for regional cooperation outside the European Union. Some of their contributions are particularly interesting because, since they are merely testimonial with virtually no real normative effect, they can remain more closely in line with the defence of individuals and fundamental rights:

> media and other actors should adhere to the highest standards of transparency regarding the source of their content and always indicate clearly when content is provided by political sources or involves advertising or other forms of commercial communications, such as sponsoring and product placement. This also applies to hybrid forms of content, including branded content, native advertising, advertorials and infotainment[137].

The European Court of Human Rights has labelled the press's function in a democratic society as that of a watchdog. According to the Strasbourg Court, the media, in their task of reporting on matters of general interest, are subject to the requirements of good faith and the lex artis of journalism[138,139,140]. Not only is none of this being done, but it needs to be taken into account in legislative initiatives of member states in the field of disinformation.
The EU countries that have legislated on this issue are all broadly following the approach of segregation and defending the status quo.

The first EU state to enforce fake news and disinformation legislation was Germany, whose NetzDG law[141] came into force on 1 October

---

137. Point 2.7. Committee of Ministers. (7 March 2018). *Recommendation CM/Rec (2018) 1 of the Committee of Ministers to member States on media pluralism and transparency of media ownership.* Council of Europe. Retrieved from <https://rm.coe.int/1680790e13>.

138. European Court of Human Rights, (2007). CASE OF STOLL v. SWITZER-LAND (Application no. 69698/01). Retrieved from <https://hudoc.echr.coe.int/eng?i=001-83870>.

139. European Court of Human Rights. (2007). CASE OF STOLL v. SWITZER-LAND (Application no. 69698/01). Retrieved from <https://hudoc.echr.coe.int/eng?i=001-83870>.

140. European Court of Human Rights. (2004). CASE OF PEDERSEN AND BAADS-GAARD v. DENMARK (Application no. 49017/99). Retrieved from <https://hudoc.echr.coe.int/eng?i=001-67818>.

141. German Federal Ministry of Justice. (n.d.). *Rules against hatred on the net - the Network Enforcement Act.* Retrieved from <https://www.loc.gov/item/global-legal-monitor/2021-07-06/germany-network-enforcement-act-amended-to-better-fight-online-hate-speech/>.

2017. "Online platforms face fines of up to €50 million for systemic failure to delete illegal content"[142] including "punishable fake news"[143]. Free speech advocates have heavily criticised it and it is having a censorial effect, with all sorts of content being removed to avoid incurring sanctions.

Shortly afterwards, France adopted a legislative package to combat disinformation[144,145]. As an example, the first significant action deriving from its application was... Twitter blocking a French Ministry of the Interior campaign for not respecting the requirements of its own legislation against fake news[146].

The major producers of structural disinformation, both on and offline, are not the targets of European legislation.

The Russian case is the most useful because it is explicit. It does not mince its words and openly expresses what the Western legislator does undercover. It punishes *blatant disrespect* for the state, its officials and Russian society and false information that looks like reliable news[148,149].

In any case, there are, of course, many liberticidal styles, and each

---

142. Echikson, W., and Knodt, O. (2018). *Germany's NetzDG: A key test for combating online hate*. CEPS Research Report No. 2018/09. November 2018. Retrieved from <https://papers.ssrn.com/sol3/papers.cfm?abstract_id=3300636>.

143. Term translated from the German *strafbare Falschnachrichten*. German Federal Ministry of Justice. (n.d.), op. cit.

144. French Republic (2018). *Organic law and ordinary law of December 22, 2018 relating to the manipulation of information*. Retrieved from <https://www.vie-publique.fr/loi/21026-loi-manipulation-de-linformation-loi-fake-news>.

145. French Republic 201. (2018) *Law No. 2018-1202 of December 22, 2018 on the fight against the manipulation of information*. Retrieved from <https://www.legifrance.gouv.fr/jorf/id/JORFTEXT000037847559/>.

146. Le Monde and AFP. (2019). 'Twitter turned down French government ad in order to comply with "information manipulation" law'. Le Monde. 2 Spril 2019. Retrieved from <https://www.lemonde.fr/politique/article/2019/04/02/twitter-refuse-une-pub-du-gouvernement-afin-de-respecter-la-loi-relative-a-la-manipulation-de-l-information_5444850_823448.html>.

147. Russian Federation. (18 March 2019). Federal Law of March 18, 2019 No. 31-FZ *On Amendments to Article 15-3 of the Federal Law. On Information, Information Technologies and Information Protection*. Official Internet portal of legal information. Retrieved from <http://publication.pravo.gov.ru/Document/View/0001201903180031>.

government in each country chooses its own[148]. There is Poland, where a law declared the expressions *Polish death camp* and *Polish concentration camp*, as well as allusions to Poland's responsibility for the Holocaust, *illegal*. However, this was later ruled as non-binding by the Polish Constitutional Tribunal[149]. Others, like Uganda, tax the use of apps because citizens can use them to lie[150]; so... they make a little money from them and limit the use of social networks to the rich.

148. Gaebee, K. (2021). *Disinformation research reveals how governments hijack & weaponize narratives to serve their political agenda.* Retrieved from <https://www.civicus.org/index.php/media-resources/media-releases/5391-disinformation-research-from-east-asia-reveals-how-governments-hijack-and-weaponize-narratives-to-serve-their-political-agenda>.

149. *Polish death camp' controversy.* (n.d.). in Wikipedia. Retrieved from <https://en.wikipedia.org/wiki/%22Polish_death_camp%22_controversy>.

150. Biryabarema, E. (4 July 2018). *Uganda leader says social media used for "lying", defends tax for access.* Reuters. Retrieved from <https://www.telecompaper.com/news/ugandan-president-says-social-media-used-for-lying-defends-tax-for-access--1251397>.

3. Fact-checking is not enough

"If your mother tells you she loves you, check it out".
-A maxim of journalism

Fact-checking, understood as the verification of newsworthy information and the debunking of untruth, is one of the founding attributes of the journalistic profession, and today, it is back at the centre of the debate to combat fake news. The spreading of information has always been accompanied by the need to verify it. It is a significant part of the journalistic profession, and this has been the case since the very beginnings of the tabloid press in the United States at the end of the 19th century and the turbulent beginnings of the following century. *Objective journalism* became popular, and with it came an appreciation of accuracy. An example is the Bureau of Accuracy and Fair Play created in 1913 by Isaac White and Ralph Pulitzer —son of Joseph Pulitzer— the New York World, considered *an innovative change*. As an example of this tradition, the term *fact-checker* was perhaps first used in a Time advertisement in 1938, although its first fact-checker was hired long before: it was Nancy Ford, hired in 1923[151].

However, we would like to highlight that in the current dynamics, most information consumers do not use or cannot access systems for verification and fact checking. So tackling the problem of disinformation only via acceding to the services of professional fact-checkers, leaving the responsibility to the people rather than to the big producers of fake news (governments, institutions, political parties, mass media, corporations, Internet platforms, large fortunes and high-impact information providers), is not balanced. And above all, it is inefficient. The thesis of this book is that verification protocols need to be applied in particular when they can still be fully effective: before viralisation, before reaching a large audience. This is also because thousands of years of dependence from information mediators can only be countered by a protracted implementation period of democratisation of the verification methods.

A study funded by the European Research Council on the consumption of fake news during the 2016 US election campaign showed that those

---

151. Fabry, M. (24 August 2017). *Here's How the First Fact-Checkers Were Able to Do Their Jobs Before the Internet*. TIME. Retrieved from <https://time.com/4858683/fact-checking-history/>.

who consumed fake news comprised less than 30% of the sample. And only half of these, 14% of all respondents, had also had contact with a fact-checking site[152].

The results of a study on fake news in Spain made by Pescanova, which seems to not be available anymore except for its summary[153], were interesting. A reasonably large sample —2,000 people— yielded the following results: six out of ten Spaniards say they know how to distinguish fake news from real news, but 86% of respondents could not distinguish fake news in the study. As for why participants claim to be able to discern whether a news item is false or not, most of them talk about the content and the credibil-ity of the information, as well as the medium or the journalist who publishes or authors it. Only 5.8% claim to check or verify information.

Another study, in this case by the German NGO Stiftung Neue Verantwortung[154], experimented by spreading fake news through Twitter followers they had bought. They came to some interesting conclusions. Firstly, that fake news is like memes: its essence is not a consistent "existence". This means blocking the source of popular fake news will not prevent it from spreading, as it is constantly re-created. Secondly, they tend to circulate within a bubble of tightly connected users, whereas refutation is carried out by a much more diverse group. Therefore, people with similar opinions seem to share the same fake news, but they have less influence on the general public.

Moreover, publishers and promoters of fact-checking initiatives acknowledge that they are perceived as *woke* by more conservative people. This coincides with the rise in disaffection towards the media, which, as is well known, is being stoked by the smear campaigns of many politicians[157].

152. Guess, A., Nyhan, B., and Reifler, J. (9 January 2018). *Selective Exposure to Misinformation: Evidence from the consumption of fake news during the 2016 U.S. presidential campaign.* Funded by the European Research Council (ERC) under the European Union's Horizon 2020 research and innovation programme (grant agreement No. 682758). Retrieved from <https://about.fb.com/wp-content/uploads/2018/01/fake-news-2016.pdf >.

153. Simple Lógica (2018). Estudio sobre el impacto de las fake news en España. <https://www.simplelogica.com/wp-content/uploads/2018/10/estudiopescanova.pdf>

154. Maebe, J. (25 July 2018). ENDitorial: The fake fight against fake news.

As occurs with the task of reporting itself[156], fact-checkers sometimes also have their editorial line or depend on certain media outlets. In other cases, companies like Facebook use them for ethicwashing, to give the appearance of concern for the accuracy of information[157]. The ecosystem is polluted by several fact-checking initiatives driven by the producers of fake news themselves[158], which are merely smokescreens.

That said, we do not want to diminish the importance of the essential work of fact-checking. Fact-checkers need to exist, will exist while information exists and we need them.

What we want to highlight is that policies that wash their hands of the problem and leave the solution to these actors alone are ill-conceived, naïve or, in most cases, fully aware that they will not solve a problem they do not wish to solve.

---

155. Guess, A., Nyhan, B., and Reifler, J. (2018) op. cit.

156. The report commissioned by the House of Commons and carried out by UK judge Brian Leveson in 2012 in the wake of the News of the World case suggested that *By far the best solution to press standards would be a body, established and organised by the industry, which would provide genuinely independent and effective regulation of its members and would be durable.* Page 1758, Leveson, B., 2012, November. *The Leveson inquiry. An inquiry into the culture, practices and ethics of the press.* Ordered by the House of Commons, presented to Parliament pursuant to Section 26 of the Inquiries Act 2005. ISBN 9780102981100. Retrieved from <https://www.gov.uk/government/publications/leveson-inquiry-report-into-the-culture-practices-and-ethics-of-the-press>. The Independent Press Standards Organisation (IPSO), an independent voluntary body, would emerge from this report. Currently, 90% of the UK press supports the proposal. This organisation has the power to conduct investigations into serious breaches of its rules and to impose sanctions on the publishing industry in an independent way. A proposal such as the IPSO could be an interesting starting point from which to consider distributed self-regulation of the mass media using the tools offered by the Internet.

157. BBC News Mundo. (4 April 2019). *Por qué verificadores de datos están abandonando Facebook en medio de su campaca contra las noticias falsas* [Why fact-checkers are abandoning Facebook amid its campaign against fake news]. Retrieved from <https://www.bbc.com/mundo/noticias-47804899>.

158. An example: The League for Cyber Threat Intelligence (CTIL), portrayed as a volunteer group, was in fact linked to government agencies in the U.S. and UK. with censorship purposes: Anwar, Hura - Digital Information World 2023. Retrieved from <https://www.digitalinformationworld.com/2023/11/top-whistleblower-makes-explosive.html>.

Codes of practice for journalism and fact-checkers — ABC of verification

Fact-checking is grounded upon the codes of good practice in journalism. Journalistic codes of ethics are shared documents containing the basic criteria for ethical journalism, including the fact-checking requirements necessary for a news story to be considered. These are codes drawn up by public law bodies and professional associations. There is not a unique document - although they often share many common features - and non-compliance is not linked to any sanctions. Fact-checking initiatives are governed by the same parameters, incorporating their own characteristics that are key to their credibility, such as the need to show a clear and transparent verification methodology that is accessible and easily reproducible.

As stated in most codes of ethics[159], and to some extent also in laws, before publishing any news item, a journalist should follow a series of steps to ensure that what they are publishing is true. In other words, a fact-checking procedure should be carried out before any publication.

Among the most common parameters in codes of ethics we find practices such as:

> • the citation of sources combined with the preservation of professional secrecy the protection of confidential sources
> • the verification of sources, including public political statements or conversations on networks, that are of public interest
> • the verification of data, official or otherwise
> • ensuring that statistics are not inflated, that the facts in question have actually taken place, that photographs are contextualised, etc.
> • the tracing of images and accounts
> • the incompatibility of mixing information with promoted content without making this explicit
> • a formal distinction between information and advertising, between information, facts and opinion and between opinion and advertising

---

159. Example: Independent Press Standards Organisation (IPSO). (n.d.). *Editors' Code of Practice*. Retrieved from <https://www.ipso.co.uk/editors-code-of-practice/>.

- transparency about media ownership
- the primacy of the information interest, of information as a fundamental
- right, and honest and ethical opinion the ability to provide prompt rectifications and facilitating the right of reply[160]

In fact-checking sources, a distinction must be made about the degree of thoroughness between perceptive sources —what the journalist sees with their own eyes or what a witness conveys to them— and elaborated sources. In this framework, some authors propose[161] to establish a hierarchy of accuracy that, for example, ignores or places political institutional sources on a lower level, as they show very evident bias. Unfortunately, in reality, they are used to being considered first-degree truthful sources.

Finally, we must consider the type of information underlying the grammatical relationship in a statement or the use of adjectives and narrative forms. For example, when a temporal relationship is passed off as a causal relationship —"After the protest, the stock market fell"— without additional data or reliable sources to back it up, or various types of linguistic tropes and narrative formulas that construe a manipulation.

However, it is well known that these codes are not always adhered to and that many media outlets, both traditional and online, are very often direct creators of or proactively complicit in the dissemination of unverified, institutionally biased, incomplete[162] or false information[163].

---

160. For examples of codes of ethics see: Parliamentary Assembly of the Council of Europe. 1993, Resolution 1003 on the Ethics of Journalism. UNESCO 1993. International Principles of Professional Ethics in Journalism, or UNESCO Declaration; - International Federation of Journalists (IFJ). 1954. Declaration of Principles on the Conduct of Journalists. Adopted by the 1954 World Congress of the IFJ. Amended by the 1986 World Congress.

161. See, for example: Capilla, J.P. (14 December 2014). *El debate epistemolygico en el periodismo informativo.* Reality and truth in news [The epistemological debate in news journalism]. Retrieved from <https://www.tdx.cat/handle/10803/287466>.

162. *Fallacy of incomplete evidence*, or cherry picking: collecting only data that confirms the thesis or ideology of the piece in question, regardless of the relevance of that data.

163. Ordway, D. M. (1 September 2017). Fake news and the spread of misinformation: A research roundup. The Journalist's Resource. Retrieved from <https://journalists-resource.org/politics-and-government/fake-news-conspiracy-theories-journalism-re-

To make it simple, it is said that there is a foolproof way to distinguish what is journalism from what is not: if you receive information from one source that says it is raining and another that says it is not, bad journalism publishes both in the name of neutrality; good journalism opens the window and checks whether it is raining.

The Internet era has brought a new qualitative leap in terms of communication tools and their capacity for reach and impact, as well as in fact-checking and verification. This makes it possible to curtail the information monopoly and create new spaces to counter it by quickly collating content and being able to respond with counter-information. This has brought with it the discrediting of the mass media and a boost for citizen journalism —be it through social media accounts, blogs, communities' forums or other similar formats— as powerful tools to scrutinise power and also to correct the asymmetry produced by the monopoly of information[164,165]. However, alongside these more positive aspects that emerged during the first phase of the Internet's expansion, there is also a reconfiguration of new monopolies that contribute to the spread of systemic propaganda for their interests. Generally, the poor state of journalism —with many honourable exceptions— is not conducive to the fight against disinformation either[166].

Checking the accuracy of information in the digital era is no longer a monopoly of journalists, or it shouldn't be. One of the inherent characteristics of democratic systems should be active public oversight of our institutions. To this end, the public should have channels to exercise this vigilance. This is why it is essential not to stick to paternalism in dealing with this disinformation issue but to bring solutions that, together with professional journalists and fact-checkers, involve citizen-distributed oversight of information. Don't worry; I'm not talking about

---

search/>.

164. Saka, E. (2017). The role of social media-based citizen journalism practices in the formation of contemporary protest movements. In *Rethinking ideology in the age of global discontent* (pp. 48-66). London, UK: Routledge. DOI https://doi.org/10.4324/9781315109008, Pages 232. eBook ISBN 9781315109008.

165. Revis, L., (10 November 2011). How Citizen Journalism Is Reshaping Media and Democracy. *Mashable*. Retrieved from <https://mashable.com/archive/citizen-journalism-democracy>.

166. Kaiser, R. G., (16 October 2014). The bad news about news. Retrieved from <http://csweb.brookings.edu/content/research/essays/2014/bad-news.html#>.

some assamblarian methodology. As said, we are in the digital era and centralised synchronic organisations are also from the past[167].

The truth is that an unfathomable amount of new content is generated on the web, while the ability to assess its reliability is still very limited, making distributed verification the only solution. It would be naïve to think that there is a magic solution, but the single logic of centralised oversight of information accuracy is an approach that, at this stage, is not only insufficient but also undemocratic and doomed to failure.

As we never tire of repeating, verification can only be effective in dismantling the dynamics of systemic disinformation if it is not limited to the media and is also applied normatively —and not merely on a voluntary basis through codes of ethics— to other institutional actors or actors that do business with information, such as in the communications of institutions, political parties and other businesses related to communication and the circulation of information. Moreover, if we take into account the fact that journalism as a profession is also a victim of the damage caused by disinformation, this approach contributes to defending journalism and restoring confidence in good journalism.

This is yet another reason to insist: it is essential that fact-checking be applied to all parties that issue or viralise information if —and only if—they are institutions or are economically profiting from it. Otherwise, a comparative disadvantage would be created with respect to those who follow and respect good practices, as they will require more time to produce their work and be more vulnerable to exposure for complying with verification.

So, let's see what we propose to tackle the problem.

---

167. Levi, Simona et al., (2021). *Proposal for a Sovereign and Democratic Digitalisation of EuropePublication Office of the European Union*. Retrieved from <https://op.europa.eu/en/publication-detail/-/publication/dae77969-7812-11ec-9136-01aa75ed71a1>.

PART 3
Let's Do The Right Thing

DISCLAIMER—WHILE READING THIS CHAPTER, ALWAYS REMEMBER: IT APPLIES ONLY TO INSTITUTIONAL COMMUNICATION AND THE COMMUNICATION PRODUCED OR DISSEMINATED FOR MONEY, NEVER FOR THE USUAL PEOPLE'S FREE SPEECH (FOR FREE).

FOLLOW THE MONEY.

1. Preventive, compulsory labelling of institutional communication and (dis)information businesses

Just as industry food products are labelled so that consumers know the composition of what they are eating, it should be possible to label information industry products (which means only influential communicators such as institutions, political parties, and anyone paying or receiving money to create or disseminate information) so that any citizen can have at least some clue about how to verify their quality.

So far, the labelling we propose is a preventive, more neutral labelling model so that anyone can reach their conclusion when accessing institutional information or information generated and viralised thanks to an economic transaction.
Let us leave free speech alone, and apply this model to institutions, information businesses and platforms.

The aim is not to establish a single, approved Truth but to set forth the objective parameters for verifying truthfulness. I.e., to apply and broaden the use of the parameters of the journalism codes of ethics.

We have outlined the types of disinformation (chapter *Modalities of falsehoods and human nature*), i.e. what we want to avoid, and the fact-checking methodologies that can be used to prevent them (chapter *Codes of practice for journalism and fact-checkers - ABC of verification*). By crossing these two elements, we aim to reverse the focus when the source is a for-profit action —by media or not— or an institution; meaning: when it is propaganda. The idea is that fact-checking should be mandatory for institutions or the communication industry before issuing the information. It seems obvious but, up till now, it is just a possibility. That must also include those who commission and receive payment for information creation or distribution. And this must happen before it enters into circulation.

So, here we propose a label/checklist of information that makes these parameters explicit. It would have to appear at the bottom of every piece of information issued by those paying or receiving payment for information and by the institutions. This would allow the reader to deduce that, for example, a piece of information whose label shows that it has not used any contrast source could be poor quality news or, more likely, propaganda for a particular side.

In short, the 'labelling' of information would make accessible something that the public is currently required to do without being provided the means to do so: fact-checking. It is said that the public is responsible for fake news because they do not verify information or check facts, when right now verifying information would be like asking someone to buy gluten-free bread in a supermarket where the food is not labelled.

We are proposing the labelling by extracting the parameters of the main Codes of Ethics:

> • Citing sources and, at the same time, protecting confidential sources
> • Verification of sources and their reliability: fact-checking; checking sources; verifying public political statements and those with networks that have a public interest; checking official and unofficial data; tracing images or accounts and identifying possible fraud; verifying with original and recognised sources, etc.
> • Cross-check all of the above with other sources
> • Formal distinction between information and advertising; between information facts and opinion; between opinion and advertising
> • Transparency of ownership
> • Transparency of methodology
> • Informative, honest and ethical interest through careful wording
> • Peer-review verification
> • Agile rectification and right of reply

TABLE

Type				
Content type	(Information) [Not necessary]	Opinion	Sponsored journalistic content	Advertising
Date of publication and date of modification	X	X	X	X
Authorship				
Authorship	X	X	X	X
Detailed which part of the information is about an item/fact that is owned or has received financial or support in kind from financial backer(s), shareholder(s) or major advertiser(s)	X	X	X	X
No astroturfing - The author/medium is also an author/beneficiary of the story	X	X	X	NO
Fact-checking				
Fact-checking	X	Only the parts relating to data and facts	Only the parts relating to data and facts	Only the parts relating to data and facts
Number [with one only source the piece cannot be considered information]. name and links to original sources used: data, statements, documents, perceptions, oral, conjecture and social construct, testimonies, whistleblowers... [protection of sensitive sources if justified]...	X	Only the parts relating to data and facts	Only the parts relating to data and facts	Only the parts relating to data and facts
If a generalisation is being drawn, samples has to be balanced, indicating the number of cases and proportions.	X	X	X	NO
Exclusivity: forbidden to claim exclusivity when a simple Google search, or other search engine, proves it is not exclusive.	X	X	X	NO
Novelty: forbidden to claim news as being new when a simple Google search, or other search engine, proves it is not.	X	X	X	NO
Algorithms				
Transparency of algorithms if used: obligation to publish the exact biases and protocols of automated operations	X	X	X	NO
Images				
Authorship	X	X	X	NO
Date and location	X	X	X	NO
Description identifying the image, unless the safety of the sources is jeopardised [justify]	X	X	X	NO
If an image has been altered, indicate the type of alterations made	X	X	X	X
Review				
Number and type of people: superior, peer, distributed review with the 1-9-90 method...	X	X	X	NO
Rectification				
Channel	X	X	X	X
To be developed further				
Motivation for excluding other notorious parameters to avoid the 'cherry picking' effect				
Motivated linguistic analysis of associations of ideas not supported by any empirical data				
Use of algorithms and auditable machine learning				

In practice, this table aims to answer simple verification questions informed by crossing known types of disinformation with codes of ethics parameters. For example: Does the information have a source or none, meaning it is made up? Is this an article about a particular company or political party paid for by that same company? Has the source been checked, or is the information simply acting as a loudspeaker for a source, publishing what they want to be published? Etc.

Label fields

Information, opinion, propaganda or advertising: who is who and what they do.

At a primary level, it should be possible to differentiate between information and non-information. Suppose the content is openly and visibly - much more than what we are used to nowadays - displayed as advertising. The verification required in that case would be the one established by advertising legislation, not journalistic fact-checking.

Complete verification is unnecessary if the content is openly stated as an opinion. The distinction between information, opinion, sponsored journalistic content, and advertising content must be clear and should not lead to confusion. Advertising does not need verification if it is presented as such, but has to respect advertising rules. Opinion does not need verification except in the aspects presented as information.

On the other hand, information issued by governments and institutions should always be considered advertising unless proven otherwise by substantiating claims with verifiable data.

Content relating to the financial backers of a media outlet or communication channel (even a political party, for example) and about actions involving these financial backers might not be considered sponsored content but advertisement. If presented as information, it should clearly state which companies or individuals mentioned in the story are in some way financial backers or shareholders of the communication channel and also how conflicts of interest, whether political, commercial, economic, financial or family-related, have been avoided.
Of course, subscribers with minimal user fees cannot be considered financial backers.

Astroturfing (when senders of information pretend not to be related to the creators or beneficiaries of the message they are sending when, in fact, they are) must also be punishable.

In short, all information broadcast and promoted by a financial or institutional transaction would have to visibly and prominently display whether it is either: verified information, or; opinion (unverified subjective content), or; sponsored content /or advertising, in which case it should indicate the actual identity of the financial backer and the amount paid for the content.

It is not about Truth; it is about the *duty of verification*

In the case of information businesses or institutional information, once information content is clearly separated from non-information content, reporting protocols must meet some standards in terms of verification, they must comply with the consolidated rules of a code of ethics, which should be a legal obligation. Once again, it is not a matter of establishing the Truth but instead of demonstrating that a duty of verification has been fulfilled: from such basic checks as a browser search to other aspects such as the dating of the piece and any modifications, details of the number and type of sources used, whether and how they have been checked, and if these sources, in turn, have applied all the protocols of verification, or the establishment of clear traceability as to how the piece has been constructed, with identified data and sources.

For example, it is interesting to know whether the information is based on:

- perceptive elements, first-hand witness or third-party report
- conjectures and social constructions, data that, while still being accurate, is based on conventions
- inferences
- modelling data prepared to be consumed such as a survey
- etc.

When statements are quoted, it should be checked whether they are consistent with the actual data. If a certain number of cases are considered to verify a hypothesis, it is possible to avoid taking an anecdote and presenting it as the norm; it is also a welcome move to justify associations of ideas that are not supported by any empirical data.

Finally, a verification protocol would have to include an agile rectification policy and efficient channels for open review.

All this sounds complicated, but in reality it is what journalists do —or should do— daily. It is just a matter of systematising it, bringing it out and applying it to more areas; it is about making it accessible, to enable distributed oversight by anyone accessing the news[168].

Moreover, when we first proposed this model, Artificial Intelligence was not there yet. But now there are already several tools that can help to apply it easily without, of course, avoiding human reviewing of AI results[169].

Since 2018 we have advocated for this model, but politicians are not listening. Meanwhile we are using tools to enforce it with our own means, despite their reluctance.

Our favourite one is the free digital tool *Skeptic Reader*[170], Your Personal Bullshit Detector for News". Skeptic Reader has a knack for detecting biases and logical fallacies in real-time. It is only to be applied to pieces claiming to be information.

Of course, the model we are proposing isn't perfect, and we should not be naïve. Conversing with colleagues[171] about our model means they express concerns that are worth keeping in mind since these rules can, of course, always be subverted.

It would be challenging to control indirect payments. There is Chomsky's

---

168. We are researching on how to increase the automatisation of the labelling model. Meanwhile, here an interesting article: https://cdt.org/insights/report-outside-looking-in-approaches-to-content-moderation-in-end-to-end-encrypted-systems/

169. Argyle, L. P., https://orcid.org/0000-0003-3109-2537, Christopher A. Bail, Ethan C. Busby https://orcid.org/0000-0002-8931-6348,+4, and David Wingate 2023 Leveraging AI for democratic discourse: Chat interventions can improve online political conversations at scale
https://www.pnas.org/doi/full/10.1073/pnas.2311627120
Stokel-Walker, C., (2023). Nature —AI tidies up Wikipedia's references— and boosts reliability
https://www.nature.com/articles/d41586-023-02894-x
Skeptic Reader - Domestic Data Streamers 2023. https://www.domesticstreamers.com/art-research/work/bullshit-detectors/

170. Skeptic Reader — Domestic Data Streamers 2023. https://www.domesticstrea-mers.com/art-research/work/bullshit-detectors/

171. Most of the examples in the following part have to be attributed to Cory Doctorow or Anne Koch.

notorious interview with Andrew Marr, where Marr told him that no one tells him what to say, and Chomsky counters that they don't have to tell him what to say, they have to make sure than only people who say the things Marr says are ever in a position to speak to the nation. At the same time, if we count indirect donations as being relevant to disclose, we mislead people by giving them the false impression that any organisation is in the pocket of a big company or individual also when actually they do not influence their activities[172].

Also, transparency is good, but transparency fatigue is real and can drown salient information in irrelevancies if it is too abundant and overwhelming. It is easy to subvert through over-compliance, so it will be impossible to tell whether someone is under the influence of specific funders.

In California, the law Proposition 69 requires companies to post warnings anywhere that you're in the presence of substances "known to the state of California to contribute to the risk of cancer." Prop 69 warnings are EVERYWHERE. Every shop, every product, every place has a warning telling you that you may be at risk of cancer. As a result, these signs are meaningless and no one pays any attention to them. In Europe, the same happens with smoking.

To avoid as much as possible these bugs, let's delimit the model: Disclosure of the income should be done, on one hand, always for the money paid or received when related to a specific item/message. On the other, we should have disclosure of incomes of the origin of the message only when relevant amount AND relevant proportion of an organisation or individual's overall income is from the same source within a year, in the last five years. And the label should be precise, in an exact place (under the information), with a precise shape to be recognisable, like in food.

We must prevent *bad actors* from harassing and SLAPPing[173] people. See for example Putin's rule that any journalist with out-of-country crowdfunding must register as a 'foreign agent' and disclose this

---

172. Next paragraphs freely inspired by a conversation with Cory Doctorow.

173. Strategic lawsuit against public participation. Retrieved from <https://en.wikipedia.org/wiki/Strategic_lawsuit_against_public_participation>.

designation before making any public statement, even an Instagram pic of their lunch; it would also let bad people escape the rule, either by making overwhelming quantities of disclosures or by structuring their funding so they slip under the disclosure rule.

Labelling will not fix ethics. It will only make things a bit better –without doubt better than now. There are organisations that can change their policy even for 1 euro or for a good word from someone famous. The majority of speakers will be influenced by power even if they receive zero from it. Our plan will not prevent this. It will just slow down the 'easy abuses', the obvious ones that at the moment can take place without any sanctions whatsoever and with no clue for people to understand their origin.

Crazier things have been seen, such as packaged foods without labelling, which was the case in the global north until less than 30 years ago. Nutritional labels provide infor-mation that helps form a purchase decision. In the United States, food nutrition labels have been mandatory since 1994, when the Nutrition Labelling and Education Act (NLEA) was passed. In Europe they have been mandatory since 2002, through the Eu-ropean Directive on Food Nutritional Information.

Of course, this can also be distorted. The US Institute of Medicine and the Centers for Disease Control published a report in 2010 on Front-of-Package Nutrition Rating Sys-tems and Symbols, which showed consumers' confusion with terms such as 'natural', 'organic', etc. Fifty-six per cent of consumers said they did not believe front-of-pack claims such as *low fat* or *high fibre*, even though these terms are regulated.

But the mere act of making the product content transparent made our diets notably healthier, almost overnight, whether we ever looked at the label or not.

Nutritional labels alone do not make a nation healthier. But nutritional labels are neces-sary for that to happen[174].

So the answer is to get on it. The sooner the better.

---

174. Mstem. (13 January 2012). *Media Diet Lessons from the Embattled History of Nutrition Labels (and the Torturous Stretching of an Innocent Metaphor)* – MIT Center for Civic Media.

2. Rules for dismantling the disinformation industry

> "We must forget the Manichean logic of truth and falsehood, and focus on the intentionality of those who lie".
>
> - Jacques Derrida

In summary, policies to combat disinformation behave like it is a new phenomenon due to the Internet and the democratisation of access to information it produces. This results in limiting freedom of speech while leaving the real promoters of systemic, democracy-damaging disinformation unpunished. These public measures focus on Internet users and embrace a logic of control and censorship by either public or private players[175]. They fail to focus on the subjects that generate and benefit most from disinformation: institutions, political parties, the media, corporations and high-worth individuals or businesses.

In response to this situation, our proposal for mandatory labelling[176] for the actors in the institutional and (dis)information business –and only them –proposes a proactive approach to correcting power asymmetries. It installs a legal obligation to check the accuracy of the information that applies to the major generators, the largest investors in (dis)information, whether they are public or private. Furthermore, the labelling obliges them to explain the information used to create a news item. This equips the public with the tools, which they currently lack, to do what is currently required of them.

As we have seen, the current legislation and policies deployed to fight disinformation often distract from the real solution, by segregating the problem to an *online* issue relating to freedom of speech.

It is important that we respect the fundamental rights of freedom of speech and information, not only because they are rights and the backbone of any state that would claim to be democratic, but also

---

175. Doctorow. C. (2019). *Speech Police: vital, critical look at the drive to force Big Tech to control who may speak and what they may say.* Retrieved from <https://memex.craphound.com/2019/06/03/speech-police-vital-critical-look-at-the-drive-to-force-big-tech-to-control-who-may-speak-and-what-they-may-say/>.

176. To reduce the workload for our legislators, we've done the bulk of the work for them here: https://xnet-x.net/es/ley-fakeyou/

because they are not the source of the problem of disinformation and fake news. If anything, they are the solution.

While our use of freedom of speech is, of course, far from perfect, it is a fundamental human right, and the way we use it will improve insofar as we are able to exercise it without asymmetries. But what we are talking about here is business, the business of content communication, and like any other business or institutional practice, there must be limits when it harms the general interest.

This is why we propose a radical shift in the approach taken to address the issue, focusing on the idea of the profit generated by disinformation. This allows us to be objective and efficient, and to move away from normative measures led mainly by the temptation to meddle with fundamental rights or to establish an official Truth.

We draw a clear distinction between the free expression of opinion and the (dis)information business. Given the general consensus that systematic disinformation is harmful to democracy, we can then conclude that there should not be an industry founded on this harmful product. We also emphasise the idea of institutional responsibility. Dereliction of their duty of care is something that is both quantifiable and punishable.

When information is offered as part of a business model (because it is offered in exchange for payment) or is offered by institutions, it is no longer a form of freedom of expression. Two obligations need then to be considered for institutions and (dis)information business: the duty to verify the truthfulness of content, and to allow verification by the recipient.

The most surprising thing, as illustrated in the previous chapter, is that there is ample, even redundant legal framework for steps in the right direction, but legislators currently ignore it. By applying certain aspects of existing regulations, extending their scope, and applying a more expansive interpretation of their objectives, it would be possible to attack the root of the problem with the existing tools without undermining rights and freedoms.

Given all this, our proposal is not radical. We therefore propose that legislators join us in getting to work on it as soon as possible[179].

How? Basically, by broadening who is subject to certain obligations and ensuring that it does cost when not complied with. In other words, the viralisation of disinformation should cease to be a viable business for the major producers of fake news, both gaining or paying money for it[177]: governments, institutions, political parties, media outlets, content platforms and companies, corporations and companies or individuals whose activities impact more than 10% of the targeted population.

Following the money works

The follow-the-money approach has proved to be effective, in particular via the action and efforts of the civil society.

The families of the victims of the Sandy Hook massacre, in which 20 children and 6 adults were killed in 2012, fought back against those who claim the shooting never hap-pened. Alex Jones, host of the InfoWars website and talk show, whose huge business model depends on maintaining his audience in a state of perpetual anxiety about power-ful, shadowy forces, has argued for years that the shooting was a *staged* government plot and that "no-one died". This spreading of false information by a *mass-media*, sup-ported by President Donald Trump too (an institution), included the addresses of the vic-tims' families. The families have received death threats and have had to move multiple times to escape the harassment. They then formed a volunteer network to track and take down the conspiracy theory videos and websites and they have filed several court cases against Alex Jones and InfoWars.

Following this series of defamation trials, Jones was ordered to pay almost $1.5bn in damages to the families of the victims. Alex Jones had to file for bankruptcy. The lawyer for the families responded that "the bankruptcy system does not protect anyone who en-gages in intentional and egregious attacks on others." Experts estimate Jones' infor-mation main company, Free Speech Systems, has generated combined net assets of between $135m and $270m.

Jones claims to offer people truths that they won't find in conventional

177. Davey, A. (2022). *Facebook Is Running Partisan Ads From "Pink Slime" Newsrooms*. Retrieved from <https://www.bloomberg.com/news/articles/2022-10-27/meta-s-facebook-is-running-partisan-ads-from-pink-slime-newsrooms-report-says>.

media, but in reali-ty, he's mainly been a big marketing machine for his true products, all kinds of oils, tinc-tures, and dietary supplements. Jones was one of the pioneers in connecting strange cures with strange political claims, but he's not the only one. Over the last decade there has been an exponential growth in influencers selling what some researchers have called conspirituality, a world view that combines New Age ideas about alternative health with the Trump era's inclination towards alternative facts, which has culminated in the QAnon and the more extreme anti-vaccine movements[178].

Sleeping Giants (SG) has been an (initially) anonymous group of people who work to combat the spread of hate speech and disinformation by discouraging advertising that appears on websites hosting this type of content. Their main strategy is to monitor and contact the companies that sponsor these websites with the goal of making them remove their advertising.

The campaign began in November 2016, shortly after Donald Trump's victory in the U.S. presidential elections, with the launch of a Twitter account that sought to boycott Breit-bart News. This is a far-right media outlet founded by Steve Bannon, which was key to the disinformation machine that led to Trump's election.

The campaign contacted the companies that advertised on Breitbart and the digital ad-vertising intermediaries that provided ads to the website, to remind them that their brands were being displayed on a portal that incited hate and promoted violence. As a result of this campaign, Breitbart lost 90% of its projected revenue for 2017, as 31 of the 34 ad exchanges withdrew.
They also successfully campaigned for advertisers to leave The O'Reilly Factor after the discovery of five sexual harassment settlements by the host Bill O'Reilly and Fox News, resulting in the cancellation of the programme.

SG theorizes that advertising can have an impact on the spread of intolerance, harass-ment and toxicity because media outlets that spread it rely on it. The automated advertis-ing system used by Google and

---

178. Manjoo, F.(11 August 2022) Alex Jones and the Wellness-Conspiracy Industrial Complex. *The New York Times.*

Facebook or AdTech in general, allows large corpora-tions to advertise on any website without companies knowing. Social media and media outlets focus on getting more clicks and money instead of moderating content, which allows fanatical or ideological disinformation groups to use these platforms to spread their message and earn money from advertising views. SG argues that it is necessary to follow the money so that polarising content no longer becomes a source of profit through advertising. Advertisers have great power to change the situation, as they can choose where to place their ads.

Nandini Jammi, one of the co-founders of SG alongside Matt Rivitz and others, has co-founded, together with Claire Atkin, Check My Ads, a consulting agency, and Check My Ads Institute, a non-profit group that focuses on investigative research. They work on the detrimental effects of broad keyword blocklisting of words like *coronavirus*, *racism*, and *immigration* on the news industry, the practice of *dark pool sales houses* where a group of unrelated publishers are misrepresented as a single entity and large American Adtech companies placing advertisements on Russian-backed disinformation websites even after the websites had been sanctioned by the US government.

Their new project aims to drain advertising from Fox News, the television company be-cause they consider it to be "the biggest defender of the Big Lie" (referring to the allega-tions of electoral fraud made by Trump after his loss in the 2022 election, which led to the January 6th attack), "the biggest purveyor of disinformation about the election and one of the most dangerous purveyors of political violence in the US."

There are many other initiatives based on the idea of following the money to stop disin-formation, as it is clear that, in most cases, it has a severe impact on societies when and because it generates business. Examples include the Boycott of The Ingraham Angle, Stop Funding Hate, and the 2018 NRA boycott.

We suggest that since civil society can make it happen, why not establish it as a rule and avoid some of these tremendously painful efforts?

More precise details on the legislation we propose can be found here [ES]: https://xnet-x.net/es/ley-fakeyou/

Let's summarise:

Who are the players?
A.- Business
A.1.- Sponsorship
A.2.- Media outlets
A.3.-Communication professionals and businesses
A.4.- Content platforms
B.- Institutions
Government[182]
Political parties
Other institutions
Private organisations with a significant impact on the population
C.- Influencers who share information and celebrities: only for those with massive impact or who receive payments
Note: Freedom of expression is intended for the anonymous public. It cannot be the same for those with power.
Yes, we believe that it is not an attack on free speech to shut down Trump's Twitter account. Rights are correctors of asymmetries where privileges exist. The privileges of some are transformed into rights for all. The role of legislation is to correct these imbalances. In the European Court of Human Rights (ECtHR) there is abundant jurisprudence[183] that establishes that politicians (and power in general) do not enjoy the same right to the protection of their reputation as private citizens since politicians, when performing a public role

---

179. Fowles, S., (2022). *The big idea: should we have a "truth law"? Today's politicians mislead with impunity – could we legislate to stop them lying?*. Retrieved from <https://www.theguardian.com/books/2022/jul/18/the-big-idea-should-we-have-a-truth-law?utm_term=62dcedf355912314de5fac8f9cb2cbd3&utm_campaign=Bookmarks&utm_source=esp&utm_medium=Email&CMP=bookmarks_email>.

as a job, must accept a greater degree of criticism and controversy than private citizens and that this must be taken into account when assessing the proportionality of restrictions on freedom of expression in relation to politicians. There is even an interesting Spanish judgement that knowing that we are lying cannot have the same degree of protection as free speech[184]. In the fight against SLAPPs, we demand the same. And here too.

What about the truth?

The information disseminated by these actors needs to be truthful by obligation. Truthfulness is not to be taken as a synonym for THE Truth. It implies the possibility of disseminating erroneous information but requires a duty of care on the part of the person informing; it means facts have to be contrasted beforehand with objective data.

Basically, we are talking about a duty of verification. The codes of conduct that apply to journalism should apply by obligation to all the mentioned players both online and offline.

Verification by the recipient

On the other hand, when we talk about allowing verification by the recipient, we are talking about making the verification process a traceable one via a mandatory labelling system for the aforementioned actors.

180. European Court of Human Rights. (2015). Case Delfi AS v. Estonia. Retrieved from <https://hudoc.echr.coe.int/fre#%7B%22itemid%22:[%22002-8960%22]%7D>.
- European Court of Human Rights. (1997). Case Gündüz v. Turkey. Retrieved from <https://hudoc.echr.coe.int/eng#{%22itemid%22:[%22001-61522%22]}>.
- European Court of Human Rights. Case Vereinigung Bildender Künstler v. Austria (2007) Retrieved from <https://hudoc.echr.coe.int/fre#%7B%22display%22:[2],%22tab-view%22:[%22related%22],%22itemid%22:[%22001-69805%22]%7D>.

181. Tribunal Costitucional (2022). Retrieved from <https://boe.es/boe/dias/2022/02/23/pdfs/BOE-A-2022-2923.pdf#BOEn>.

The responsibility for the accuracy of the labelling should be borne by both those who pay for that information to become viral, and those who receive

payment. Its application must be accompanied by a strict sanctioning regime, as happens with food. This has three main objectives:

– To check whether the verification has actually been carried out
– To allow anyone who reads the information to check the verification for themselves
- To generate a positive chilling effect in improving the quality of information

About Transparency

As mentioned above, to avoid the model being used for repression or subverted through over-compliance, let's delimit it:

Disclosure of the income should be done, on the one hand, always for the money paid or received when related to a specific item/message. On the other hand, we should disclose the income of the message's origin only when the relevant amount AND the relevant proportion of an organisation or individual's overall income from the same source within a year in the last five years are available. And the label should be precise, in a precise place (under the information), with a precise shape to be recognisable, as with food.

Civil society has been fighting for years to declare as a fundamental right the right of access to information, not only public information, but information in the public interest.

We need to know who is behind the media and political parties as well as the major sponsors of the information and viralisation that takes place both online and offline. This data needs to be public and kept up-to-date.

Specifically, we need to establish an obligation to disclose the details of payments made and received for communication, linking the amounts paid to the exact content of the items/services (messages, publications, bots, banners, posters, campaigns, adtech, positioning, content creation and use of algorithms, etc.). This applies to each of the services contracted or performed by in-house teams.

As for the use of algorithms, data, AI and the impact of technological processes on information and its viralisation, we must first start out with the protection of human rights:

1/ Privacy should be by design and by default, with no information personalised by default. This should only be optional, with data provided voluntarily by the user.

How?

2/ With the explicit consent of the user: freely given through the browser settings or similar, consent that is not void, not forced. No mass opt-in. No dark-patterns.

3/ Eliminating third-party tracking: Data is not to be extracted from users; only data provided freely should be used to display personalised information. It bears noting that personalised advertising is not the problem. This already exists: for example, in TV advertising by time slot, in a magazine by type of topic, etc. The problem lies in the tracking of personal data and its use for profiling.

4/ The obligation of interoperability (the possibility for users to take information from one platform to another) aimed at addressing consent fatigue, not at transferring data to other services.

5/ Regulation should NOT differ between online and offline or for political, issue-based and commercial advertising and content, nor should it apply only for specific periods of time (election campaigns).

Within this framework, the programming parameters of algorithms should be public and included in this labelling: how a social network, a search engine or others position certain content for the users, even if it is not promoted. We need to see how the network, the search engine or others decide what in their opinion is relevant for users; how adtech, be it marketing, political or other, is programmed; how bots, deepfakes and any other modification or intervention using technology should be brought to light, just as we have indicated that manipulations carried out without the use of technology (cherry-picking, etc.) should be brought to light.

As for bots and automated viralisation, in reference to a broader scope relating to algorithmic governance in general, Tim Wu, professor at the Faculty of Law at Columbia University, author of *The Attention Merchants: The Epic Struggle to Get Inside Our Heads*[182], suggests that

> "a simple legal remedy would be a 'Blade Runner' law that makes it illegal to deploy any programme that hides its real identity to pose as a human. Automated processes should be required to state, "I am a robot." When dealing with a fake human, it would be nice to know"[183].

Some of this has been weakly regulated in the EU Digital Service Package (DSA-DMA), GDPR and AiAct. We don't enter in to details since it is so far from done.

Online and OFFLINE

It needs to be stressed again that such actions must not only affect press and online intermediaries (content platforms and social networks) but also the whole investment chain. Focusing regulation on online platforms, as currently mostly happens, has very clearly resulted in those platforms safeguarding their commercial interests and reducing their legal risks by applying the curtailment of user's freedom of expression, resulting in moves towards a single acceptable pensée unique and automated censorship.

---

182. Wu, T., (2016). *The Attention Merchants: The Epic Struggle to Get Inside Our Heads.* Knopf Publishing Group. ISBN-10: 0385352018. ISBN-13: 978-0385352017.

183. Wu, T., (2017). *Please Prove You're Not a Robot.* New York Times. Retrieved from <https://cacmb4.acm.org/opinion/articles/219417-please-prove-youre-not-a-robot/full-text>.

There is nothing new about this dynamic: since the dawn of time, governments have used intermediary structures to enforce surveillance and censorship policies. Control over what people say and do is often delegated to private parties. They ensure that their users do not commit acts that upset the incumbent powers, and in return, they receive a wider margin of movement and freedom for their business. This is how "copyright" (copy+right, the right to print for publishers) was born, and this is exactly what is happening now[184].

The incumbent powers cry foul and baulk at the evils of, for example, Meta and the entire Internet; Meta issues an apology and vows to be the guarantor of truth on the Internet from now on. And everyone is happy. Those in power can continue to lie and Meta can continue with its walled garden, but with an advantageous ethicwashing for both: Meta reduces the visibility of 'unofficial' media on its platforms, which means that blogs and the independent press —the competitors for the mainstream opinion and the status quo— are de facto excluded from the platform, as journalists in several countries are already denouncing[185], while Meta and other GAFAM are accepted as the main advisors of the legislator about digital. The deal is win-win.

The dichotomy actually lies here: unlike in the US, where restrictions on the ability of mediators to moderate user content may implicate the First Amendment rights, which are also protected under Section 230 of the Communications Decency Act, which affirms the non-liability of service providers for user content[186], other tendencies, like in the EU, take the opposite tack. This is reminiscent of the historical approach in the time of the Inquisition[187].

More than half a millennium ago, in the mid 1400s, a technology emerged

184. Levi, S., (2021). *Inventions, Democracy, Copyright and Censorship (I)* Xnet. Retrieved from <https://xnet-x.net/en/inventions-democracy-copyright-censorship/>.

185. Dojcinovic, S. (2017). *Hey, Mark Zuckerberg: My Democracy Isn't Your Laboratory,* New York Times. Retrieved from <https://www.benton.org/headlines/hey-mark-zucker-berg-my-democracy-isn%E2%80%99t-your-laboratory>.

186. EFF. *Section 230 of the Communications Decency Act.* Retrieved from <https://www.eff.org/issues/cda230>.

187. infoLibre. (14 May 2021). Ante el inminente #Decretazo sobre copyright. *infoLibre.* Retrieved from <https://www.infolibre.es/opinion/plaza-publica/inminente-decretazo-copyright_1_1197653.html>.

that was new to the *West*: the printing press 176. Something similar had existed in China since the 7th century, but in China, Japan and later Korea, Russia, and the Ottoman Empire, socio-political conditions were not conducive to its expansion at various social levels.

In the West, its expansion generated transformations that led to access to knowledge, the debate of ideas and the emergence of new currents of thought. It was a catalyst at a time of upheaval and discontent and changed the methods of reasoning.

By making incompatible views on the same subject much more accessible, it stimulated criticism in general and criticism of authority in particular. After little more than 50 years the established powers, which had been caught off guard, began a frantic fight to the death against access for the people to this tool and its proliferation. Mainly as part of the Inquisition, the use of this technology for anyone who was not part of the power represented a via crucis of prohibition, death and destruction for 300 years. Yet, they never managed to stop access to printed press. Now we have a *new* technology, the Internet, with a little over 50 years of mass dissemination, which once again allows the expansion of knowledge and the creation of distributed networks, allowing the democratisation of the ways in which we generate and access information.

Alarmingly, we can see history repeating itself. The offensive against this tool is very similar to that experienced by humanity half a millennium ago. We are witnessing an alliance between power and both old and new monopolies for the control of technology and the flow of information against freedom of expression and access to information.

The Inquisition held publishers responsible if prohibited content was published, i.e. it made them the guarantors of the *legality* of what was published. In return, publishers could keep the economic rights of the authors, a practice that proved so successful that it still survives today. This is copyright, the right to make copies.

Their goal is not to stop disinformation but to avoid criticism against them.

In the US, according to the Congressional Research Service[188], there are at least three possible frameworks for analysing governmental restrictions on the ability of social media sites to moderate user content:

> First, social media sites could be treated as state actors who are themselves bound to follow the First Amendment when they regulate protected speech. (…) The second possible framework would view social media sites as analogous to special industries like common carriers or broadcast media. (...) This would imply that if special aspects of social media sites threaten the use of the medium for communicative or expressive purposes, courts might approve of content-neutral regulations intended to solve those problems. The third analogy would treat social media sites like news editors, who generally receive the full protections of the First Amendment when making editorial decisions. If social media sites were considered to be equivalent to newspaper editors when they make decisions about whether and how to present users' content, then those editorial decisions would receive the broadest protections under the First Amendment. Any government regulations that alter the editorial choices of social media sites by forcing them to host content that they would not otherwise transmit or requiring them to take down content they would like to host could be subject to strict scrutiny. A number of federal trial courts have held that search engines exercise editorial judgment protected by the First Amendment when they make decisions about whether and how to present specific websites or advertisements in search results, seemingly adopting this last framework.

> Which of these three frameworks applies will depend largely on the particular action being regulated. Under existing law, social media platforms may be more likely to receive First Amendment protection when they exercise more editorial discretion in presenting user-generated content, rather than if they neutrally transmit all such content. In addition, certain types of speech receive less protection under the First Amendment. Courts may be more likely to uphold regulations targeting certain disfavoured categories of speech such as obscenity or speech inciting violence. Finally, if a law targets social media conduct rather than speech, it may not trigger the protections of the First Amendment at all.

In reality, the solution to disinformation lies in expanding democracy, and once again there is no need to reinvent the wheel. What needs to be democratised is the prioritisation of content, giving people the authority to control it and to know also what they are not seeing and what they are missing. If media, authorities, platforms, power in general

---

188. Brannon, V.C. (27 March 2019). *Free Speech and the Regulation of Social Media Content.* R45650. Congressional Research Service. Retrieved from <https://crsreports.congress.gov/product/pdf/R/R45650>.

online and offline prioritise content on the basis of self-serving criteria to increase people's engagement, i.e. stay longer in a walled garden spurred on by hate, fear and anger, they are acting as publishers, so they should be subject to publishing laws and be held accountable. But it is more democratic to do the opposite: not allow them to be editors, prioritise and trap us, and let users be in control[189]. We can learn to do this, since otherwise our right to information is infringed.

Conclusion — To Combat Disinformation: More Democracy

What would we have done if we had been present during the great changes of the past? It is easy to realise that the invention of the Internet has brought similar issues to the invention of the printing press. If we do not react promptly, as a society, we face centuries of inquisition, propaganda, control and censorship by those who do not want information technology democratically accessible.

We hope this book can be useful each time we are told from a parliamentary source, a high-level committee or a media outlet that we are the cause of disinformation. Let it serve as a lightning rod against moralistic technophobes and self-interested manipulators who fabricate or endorse propaganda surrounding fake news and against the democratisation of technologies.

Don't blame the people; don't blame the Iinternet; blame the power.

---

189. Davis, W., (2012). Texas Transformed Social Media Platforms Into 'Common Carriers,' AG Argues. Policy Blog, *MediaPost*. Retrieved from <https://www.mediapost.com/publications/article/368940/texas-transformed-social-media-platforms-into-com.html>.

www.ingramcontent.com/pod-product-compliance
Lightning Source LLC
Chambersburg PA
CBHW061148160726
48006CB00038B/2310